Where are they going?

Where does Indian education
take them?

Jeyapandian Kottalam

Released as eBook on July 8, 2024

To download

https://drive.google.com/file/d/1JwZn3k1DOJIQdEPp2QwMcltbZ lvFfYPM/view?usp=drive_link

The Tamil version of this book

https://drive.google.com/file/d/1qZA_-EF5W7hpmDKmkvQsaFZ1- 9ITwkPY/view?usp=drive_link

List of writings by author

https://drive.google.com/file/d/1K-v- 0eeapcdhPKPbsCuU9yhvm8rV_0RQ/view?usp=drive_link

jkottalam@gmail.com
https://www.facebook.com/kottalam

Contents

1 Introduction

Your lifestyle is simple. Your living environment is trashy and dusty. You may not know where your next meal is coming from. You may not have good clothing to wear. And yet, you adore your children, dress them up in school uniform, comb their hair, hug them, and send them off to school with their bags of books. Your hopes are high that their life will blossom because of their education.

When they return from school you look forward to them eagerly. You imagine that they are returning home with treasures of knowledge. You have the happy thought that they are walking towards a prosperous future.

On the other hand, if you are well to do, you send your children to private schools teaching in English. You have the happy thought that your children are getting an education that is superior to poor children.

Does your dream in fact come true, in either case? You send your children to school with the firm belief that educators and the government officials in charge of education are smart people and they are guiding your children in the right direction. But have you ever verified this belief? Have you ever surveyed what benefits children receive from education?

There are a few children who have succeeded in their education. You praise them. But there are many who did not. What do you say about them? Since they did not excel in studies, do you consider them less intelligent? If your children cannot study, have you ever thought that this could be the fault of the educational system?

Children are not only a treasure for parents, but for society too. They are the human resources for a society. Here society may be your town, may be Tamilnadu, may be India, or it may even be the world. It is because of these children's knowledge, thoughts, and ethics that society at every level is going to prosper. If a society is to be elevated, it is essential to educate and guide the children of that society in the right direction. This is what education should achieve.

What is the true purpose of education? Does the education in India and Tamilnadu achieve that purpose today? Are the government officials authoring educational policies smart? Even if they are, do they set up the educational system for the benefit of all children, or for the benefit of their own children? Do they provide the knowledge needed for your children, or do they inculcate the children in principles favorable to themselves?

We are going to address such questions in this book. Let us think about what is good for the future of your children. Guiding children in the right direction is ultimately the parents' responsibility. Even if you delegate the responsibility to educators and the government, shouldn't you ensure that they carry out the task properly?

You may ask whether it is right to raise such questions. The teaching profession is divine. Can we insult it? Is it proper to diminish the respect students and parents have for teachers? These are fair questions. However, just as it is possible for a thief to enter an unguarded house, it is possible for unethical practices to enter the educational system with the expectation that education is holy, and no one would question the system. It is the responsibility of the citizens to ensure that this does not happen.

Teachers mostly consider education divine and want to impart knowledge to students with a sense of responsibility. But, at the same time, there are those who utilize education as a commercial product to make money. We shall see their methods in detail in this book. Further, we shall see that education can be used as a tool and a weapon for political purposes and to exert power over others and some do use it in that manner.

Current educational system in India is favorable to the rich and the urbanites. It depresses the poor and rural population further. It does not provide any opportunity to educate and economically elevate the children of the oppressed sections of society. It piles opportunities to the children of the powerful and ruling class. In this book, we will learn about this educational system, its effects on people, and what you can do to change it.

Since the education system in India provides opportunities for the upper class and not for the smart people, India is lagging in scientific research and technological development. To change this, qualified people should be selected from all sections of society without discrimination based on caste, religion, language, economic status, domicile; and provided higher education for placement in responsible positions in the country. If this is done, the thinking capacity of the country will increase, and the country will improve on many fronts.

I will describe an alternative method of education for this purpose. The existing system can be converted to the new system in phases. This is a long-term plan. It may take decades to fully implement it.

2 What is education?

What should be the purpose of education? Let us think about this a bit.

2.1 Education today

When asked about education, most parents of today would answer that it provides their children with the qualifications needed to get a job and make their future comfortable. Most middle-class families think that the aim of education is to obtain good grades and good grades will get their children good jobs. If everyone's goal is to get a job, have you ever thought about who provides those jobs?

Most large corporations in India today are foreign corporations. These foreign corporations consume a large portion of your children's labor. Additionally, some children even go abroad.

When your child (son or daughter) grows older, why can't they become the owner of such a company? Why can't that company be a fully Indian company? Even if it is not a large corporation, young people can be encouraged to get involved in small industries and grow over time. How should they be prepared now to reach such a goal? What kind of education is needed for it? Does the country provide such an education?

There is nothing wrong with some going abroad. But can everybody go? Is there space for everyone in other countries? Shouldn't you be improving life in your society? Shouldn't you make your country as prosperous as those other countries?

All right, let us say that you don't care about society or country: you just want your children to do well. There is nothing wrong with that either. It is natural that everyone has selfish and social interests. Even from an individual's perspective, the number of employment opportunities in the kinds of corporations mentioned above is small compared to the population of India. It is impossible for everyone to get such a job. Not all students can study well enough to get good grades in school. Even if they do, can everyone get first rank? Only one can have the first rank. Only some can have top ranks. Since jobs are a few and jobseekers are many, companies can only employ the top few. Because of this, there is heavy competition in education and employment.

If studying and getting a job is your child's only goal, what if they do not study so well? Don't you need an alternative plan? Children who do not score well are seen as not smart, not hard working, or both. This greatly affects their confidence and self-worth. Society looks at them as worthless and hence they become so.

If your child is not interested in studies, or does not get good grades, they should be prepared for some other profession or business. Where can they get the education for it? Do schools today provide it?

Education today does not develop children's thinking and problem-solving skills. It conducts the competition "let is see who can memorize the best what I am saying". Will this develop their minds? Will it sharpen their intelligence? Will it improve their thinking ability? The net effect of education at present is that those who succeed in this competition get jobs in companies. In other words, the effect of education is to conduct a competition among students and choose the most suitable servants for corporations. It stamps others as "useless" and discards them.

2.2 Objectives of education

Your children in school today are going to live for about ninety years more. You cannot always be with them and guide them. If you steer your child towards the profession that looks good today, who knows how things will change in ninety years!

The fundamental objective of education should be to make children knowledgeable, develop their intelligence, and train them to analyze problems arising in life and to solve them rationally. If parents make children knowledgeable, children will utilize that knowledge to adapt to situations. If necessary, they will learn new skills and professions.

In addition to making children great thinkers, parents should find out their interests and involvements at an early age and guide them into professions where they can naturally excel. Guiding them into working in corporations is a narrow outlook.

Caring parents would ask what if the child's natural interest and involvement is in herding cows. The reason this question arises is that the cattle industry is not respected in India and cattle farmers do not get fair remuneration. In America, cattle farming is as respected as any other profession and these professionals lead a comfortable life. Education should bring about a social change such that all professions are respected and there is equality among all people.

Everyone born in the world makes a living by some profession. If someone interested in herding cows is forced to become an engineer, in the end they would end up as a cowherd. One of my relatives has been very interested in goats, cows, and chickens. Even as a boy he used to take a lot of pleasure rearing them and caring for them. His parents sent him to college. After the studies, he now has four or five milk cows and is selling milk. He rears chicken and provides meat and eggs to society. It is true that this man would not be as rich as a software engineer. But even if he was forced into the engineering profession, he would not have made a good engineer, because his mind would not be in it. You can find numerous examples like this if you just look around yourself.

People understanding social affairs is also part of education. Education is something that continues for life. India is nominally a democratic country. A prerequisite for democracy to function well in a country is that its people should understand the process of democracy. If a society were to function properly following rules and regulations, its people should understand how the rules and regulations operate. Education should provide the knowledge and skills necessary for solving social problems in addition to those arising from personal life.

Food, shelter, and clothing are fundamental needs for human life. After these needs are satisfied, the human mind wants to engage in other activities. Then, arts such as literature, music, and painting give happiness to humans. These happy thoughts refine human minds and keep antisocial thoughts from arising. For this reason, education should cultivate an appreciation for the arts.

Education should train all members of society to follow ethical principles. This too prevents people from engaging in antisocial activities.

Education is the conductance of knowledge obtained by one generation from its experiences in science, politics, arts, ethics, etc. to the next generation and exchange of such knowledge with other societies.

Let us look at the points mentioned above in more detail.

2.3 Intelligence and knowledge

The **intelligence** of a person represents the ability of the person to absorb **knowledge** through education, to understand complex concepts clearly, and to solve problems effectively with the knowledge so obtained. Here, solving problems denotes not only solutions to mathematical problems but also problems arising from life and society.

People are of different kinds. We cannot expect everyone to have the same degree of intelligence. It is true that people of higher intelligence can get more knowledge and a better life. This is what Thiruvalluvar also said in

வெள்ளத் தனைய மலர்நீட்டம் மாந்தர்தம்

உள்ளத் தனைய துயர்வு (Thirukkural 595)

Roughly, it means that the height of one's achievement is determined by one's mind just as the height of lily is determined by water level. If a person has low intelligence naturally, it is not their fault. We cannot respect them any less. Respecting all as equals is one of the good nature of humans. Further, since this is a natural state, we cannot increase one's intelligence by scolding him.

When Thiruvalluvar said mind, he meant not only intelligence, but he included all aspects of the mind. Intelligence is one of them. Others are orientation and inspiration. Different people are interested in different areas. We call this an individual's orientation. Among people of the same intelligence and orientation, those who are inspired more can achieve more. Inspiration is internal, and no one can give it from outside. Thus, we can understand the full meaning of "as high as the mind".

Education should develop every student's intelligence to the best of his or her ability. One curriculum may not be beneficial for every student. Everyone has different abilities, interests, and inspiration. If the teacher tries to take them all in a particular direction, those students with interests in that direction would be successful and others would fail. Today's education is oriented towards joining corporations or becoming professionals such as physician, engineer, lawyer to earn money. Not all children are oriented to earning money is also a fact regrettable by parents. But everyone needs education.

Education should have the broad perspective of making every student as best a thinker as possible. Education should develop problem-solving skills. It should provide the skills and attitude to take responsibility for the issues arising in life, analyze the problems, think accordingly, and make decisions without attributing them to fate or gods. These skills are useful to analyze social needs, think about the causes of social problems, and seek solutions. Therefore, education should be for the sake of education, not for getting jobs.

2.4 Social justice and equality

Why should we think low of retail business, farming, animal husbandry and such? Children with natural skills in these areas arrive at these professions at the end. We don't need to torture them by sending them all on the same path. Forcing children against their interests not only wastes time and effort but is greatly detrimental to their self-confidence. Since society thinks less of children who do not get grades in school, they lose self-esteem. This is bad for their mental health.

There is a good reason for parents not liking their children being in the profession of retail shop, farming, or hairstyling. Society does not respect these professionals; they do not get significant income.

At present in India, medical professionals are valued highly, and haircutting professionals are valued lowly. When I first came to America, I was shocked to see how expensive it was to get a haircut. Now I understand. Just like every physician and engineer has a family, the haircutter also has a family. A minimum income is required for the fundamental needs of that family. In America too, physicians earn more than hairstylists. Yet, most people live with fundamental facilities. Government helps those who are below a baseline.

Society needs all professions. It needs people to perform all jobs. When that is the case, why does society grant higher value and higher income to certain professions? Those who go to the office wearing white shirts without getting dirty are respected better and they lead comfortable lives. Fisherfolks suffer in poverty. Animal farming to supply society with meat and milk is considered an inferior profession. Farmers who feed society are considered unskilled.

Do you know why? What is the reason for this situation to exist in India only? Think! It is a historical tradition that lowered caste people are engaged in such professions. It is a black mark – no, a black splotch, a black screen - in Indian history that people were arranged in hierarchy ranked by caste. Nowhere in the world has such injustice occurred. The high caste people prescribed which caste should be engaged in which profession. Professions such as haircutting, laundering, and ploughing were considered lower and those who did them lower castes. Getting educated and chanting to the gods were the jobs for the higher castes.

When caste and profession were inseparably united, the work done by lower castes was also considered lower. These workers lived in poverty. This attitude keeps some professions at a lower status even after we have reached (or we think we have reached) the state where anyone can be in any profession.

True education should change this attitude. Everyone should be educated to value all professions. Equality should be established. People should become equal not only by caste, but also by profession. All laborers and professionals should have a baseline lifestyle. The situation that wearing a white shirt and going to the office is the only way to a comfortable life should change.

Inculcating the idea that no profession is inferior should be an objective of education. At the present state, we are unable to see washing clothes and software engineering as of equal status. This attitude has arisen in us by social habit. This can only be changed gradually. But its ultimate achievement should be the goal of education. Educational policies should devise steps to achieve this goal.

Here I am talking about equality, not about communism. What is the difference between the two? Equality is everyone having equal opportunities for betterment according to their intelligence, orientation, and inspiration without any artificial barriers such as caste, domicile, and economic status. Communism is sharing facilities of life equally without regard to individual contributions.

Equal education is education for all; inclusive of all. It benefits everyone. It doesn't elevate a section of society neglecting others. It provides knowledge to all and trains them in any profession they are interested in. Corporate employment and professional development are side effects to those with such orientations.

கற்க கசடற கற்பவை கற்றபின்

நிற்க அதற்குத் தக (Thirukkural 391)

"Live as you have learned" he said, not learn only to make a living.

Education should prepare every member of society to contribute in some way to society. The government should devise educational policies to this end and implement them. In such a society, there won't be stealing, cheating, begging, or violence.

2.5 Social affairs

If we think about education beyond employment and lifestyle, clearly education should sharpen the intellect and develop the mind. Education should provide every individual with a broad world knowledge according to their desire. It should encourage thoughts on where the country and world are going, what the meanings of world affairs are, how we contribute to society, what effect our contributions have, how we can contribute better to improve ourselves and our society. It is not enough to keep doing what others tell us to do.

Why should we think about society? "Is it my job to elevate society?" one may think. Yes, it is also your job! Society is a combination of all of us. No one lives isolated. Everyone lives in a society. We share natural resources. We make common facilities for ourselves.

In the old days, everyone drew water from a well in the middle of the town. Who dug the well? The townsfolk must have done it. It is a social task. Nowadays, the local government installs water pipes and supplies water to every house. If this is an uncorrupt government, it collects a tax equal to the expense involved in providing the people with such facilities. This is the same social task in another form. Facilities such as roads, bridges, dams, schools, transportation, and police are also government tasks. It is for this purpose a system called government arose. It is a right of every citizen to receive benefits from such facilities. It is also the responsibility of every citizen to see that these tasks are performed properly. This is why everyone should think about society. This is also about your life.

Just like we care about our family, we care about our town. The same way we should care about our state, our country, and our world. It is the job of education to make everyone know how these social activities function, their budgets, and the process for checking and correcting any irregularities in them.

If society were to follow rules and regulations, its people should understand how the rules and regulations operate. People will receive the benefits of the law only if they understand how the police and the courts operate. If they do not understand, people are under the control of policepersons, lawyers, etc. Even if they do not know the intricacies of the law, they should understand common aspects of the law such as the traffic rules. This is also the responsibility of education.

In principle, there is democratic rule in India as provided by the constitution. That is, the government consists of representatives of the people. To elect representatives, everyone beyond a certain age can vote. For such a democratic system to function properly, the people should understand well the meaning of their votes, the duties and responsibilities of those who receive the votes and get elected, the consequences of such elections, the long-term effects of such consequences. Only then, people can elect a government suitable for the development of the country. Education should provide such knowledge to everyone.

2.6 Appreciation for the arts

Fundamental human needs are food, dwelling, and clothing. We need a certain amount of wealth to obtain these. It is true that the poor who are struggling to fulfil these fundamental needs cannot think beyond it. But, after these needs are fulfilled, what do we do? Under those situations, literature and art provide happiness to the human mind. The arts can engage the minds in a pleasurable world view and prevent antisocial thoughts.

When we think of literature most of us think of ancient Tamil literature. But literature goes beyond poetry and fiction. It includes literature providing different kinds of knowledge. Books on arts such as music, dance, and painting as well as books on scientific topics are included in literature. One can choose something attractive from these for a hobby.

Some may be interested in ancient literature. I need not mention that Tamil has a long rich literary tradition. Some may get interested in mathematical puzzles. The natural world, the organisms in it, and their lifestyles may be fascinating to some others. Some may be curious about how the universe appeared and evolved. Human relations in a society and interactions among societies may attract the attention of some people. Philosophical questions such as who I am and what the meaning of this life is can occupy some minds.

Moreover, there are performing arts such as music, dance, and painting. In addition to getting pleasures by seeing and hearing these arts, we can also create them. We can read about them too. We can consume the treasures of art generated by artists over many centuries. In such art, there are simple arts and fine arts. For example, let us take music. Kuthuppaattu (குத்துப்பாட்டு) is simple music. It is based on the homogeneous simplicity of a single rhythm and melody. In contrast, there are broad and intricate patterns at several levels in the melodies and rhythms of Carnatic music. Since the deeper parts of our minds and intellect are involved in enjoying these patterns, these can provide more pleasure. Because of this, we call arts like Carnatic music and Bharatnatyam fine arts.

Anyone who gets involved in Tamil literature, Carnatic music, or science will never get bored in life, because one lifetime is not enough to completely consume any one of these. No matter how much you take they never diminish.

Reading and being involved in fine arts are educational activities. To the extent that we get involved in these activities our knowledge expands; we can use our intellectual skills to that extent.

தொட்டனைத் தூறும் மணற்கேணி மாந்தர்க்கு

கற்றனைத் தூறும் அறிவு (Thirukkural 396)

This Kural says that just as a spring yields more when water is drawn, the human mind expands to the extent it is exercised to learn.

So, education should provide the minds with the exercises to think. It should create the habit of reading books of interest and induce a curiosity for it. Then creative thoughts can arise in human minds.

I should mention here about the sexual art. Just as creating music and painting for the enjoyment of others is art, giving pleasure to another person is also an art. Just as the artist is happy to see when others enjoy it, the provider is happy to see the other person enjoying the pleasure he or she gives. This art too helps to keep people happy and healthy.

2.7 Ethics

Ethics arises by itself from the good nature of people. Respecting each other, not finding inferiority or superiority among people, respecting others' rights are ethical principles. This is different from morality. Morality is following rules prescribed by someone else as to what is good and what is bad.

It may be difficult to distinguish between ethics and morality. Both talk about good and bad. Both agree on most issues. The fundamental difference between the two is that ethics arise from one's mind and morality comes from outside based on somebody else's rules. It may be the Bible, the Quron, the Bhagavat Gita, or your grandmother who said it. Further, what one person's grandma says may be different from what another's grandma says.

Suppose that someone is involved in an accident and lying on the road. Taking them to the hospital or fetching medical help is ethical. Running away with the jewelry on her neck and hands is unethical. Your grandma may also have said "helping is good and running away with jewelry is bad". But if you help only because your grandma has said so, you are following moral rules. If you do what your mind says, you are following ethics. The person who steals due to poverty or some other reason also knows that it is wrong.

In some situations, ethics and morality may contradict. For example, your grandma may have said the moral rule that a person of lower caste may not sit on a chair while a person of higher caste is sitting on the floor. But we cannot derive any reason for this from human nature. There is no reason except your grandma said so.

As another example, it may be a morality in one society that a widow must not remarry. In another society, the morality may be that any person can marry any number of persons one after the other. The latter is also ethical. One person having a married life with more than one person simultaneously leads to some family problems and social issues; so, this is considered unethical in most societies. The laws of a society are mostly based on ethical principles.

Ethics can be defined as something that does not cause any harm and does not interfere with individual rights. That is, everyone has the right to live their life as they wish without causing any harm to themselves, others, or society. Note that inaction can sometimes be harmful and hence is unethical. For example, not helping the injured is harmful to the injured. Expecting others to live according to one's wishes is also unethical. For example, you may not like an unmarried woman having a child. But if she likes it, it is her right. Ethical principles apply equally to everyone without any distinction of caste, religion, economic status, domicile, gender, educational status, etc.

Education should encourage ethical thoughts acceptable to all people. It should provide the maturity to think ethically. Education should make people understand the social effects of unethical thoughts and actions. People should care about their society at all levels as they care about themselves, their families, and their towns.

A society without ethical thinking will decay. Its members will take pleasure and pride in being rogues and cheats. A society would not prosper if people cheated each other. If one section of society intends to become rich by obtaining wealth from another section, such a society would not produce anything; but due to maintenance expenses the total wealth of the society would diminish. Spending without income would depress the economy of the society and ultimately the society will perish.

2.8 Education as transfer of knowledge

Education is not something we get from schools and colleges only. In general, education is the transfer of our ancestors' experience from one generation to the next. This education can happen at home and in society. Schools and colleges only provide the environment for such education.

The country called India was created from people who were in individual states or societies at historical times. This is a democratic country. In this country, all kinds of people are equal. If this equality should persist, it should manifest itself in all aspects of life, especially in education.

People of different societies can have different experiences. When these societies come together, education should enable societies to transfer the knowledge obtained from their experiences among themselves. If a situation exists where the experiences and cultural values of a certain society are to be followed by all other societies, it means that one society imposes its values on other societies. That is dominance.

To put it explicitly, the education that imposes the values of high caste Hindus on others creates contradiction in society. An education that imposes a particular language on states speaking other languages causes social turbulence.

Education is knowing about all classes of people in society, learning from their varied experiences, and sharing their knowledge with other classes.

Education transfers experiences in two directions. One is the transfer between generations. The other is transfer among societies. By this transfer, every society can learn when needed from other societies and take what they want without losing their identity and cultural values. In other words, education should be a means to take what is needed without impositions.

If leaners can learn what they want as they want, their thinking skills will manifest. People will get involved in areas of their interests and take professional initiatives. They will have a chance to evolve as employers rather than just employees.

True education is beyond social strata. It does not differ based on caste, religion, language, wealth, domicile, parents' educational status, etc. Everyone should have equal opportunities in getting educated according to their intelligence and interests.

In India there are many divisions based on caste, religion, language, culture, morality, values, etc. Every division should not only get an education but also have a chance to provide their cultural values and language to other divisions. All societies should be valued as equal, and everyone should contribute to education. This is an education policy based on society.

When people think about how to solve issues arising from society and how to fulfil society's needs, they arrive at solutions using their intelligence. Here, keep firmly in mind that people includes both men and women. Don't forget that it represents all divisions such as castes and religions. **'Intelligence' is the natural curiosity and ability for people to acquire knowledge. The total of solutions and experiences obtained with this intelligence is called 'knowledge'. Transferring this knowledge from one to another is 'education'.**

The science, technology, electronic devices, medicine, economic principles, sociology, arts that we find today all arose on this basis. They have evolved over a long time and developed into school curriculum. It is only natural that this development will continue because society keeps generating new issues and needs. We should not be satisfied with memorizing existing knowledge. We should recognize society's new needs and our youngsters should think about solutions. We call this process **research**. Education should develop thinking ability and attitude to research.

If you leave recognizing the needs of your society to other societies or countries, they will undertake the research on what your society needs, make products that you need and sell it to you and sell the services you need. Their economy will grow and yours will diminish. Moreover, if you train your children to do what they are told without training their thinking ability, the other society will utilize them as laborers.

3 Language and education

Education is not only what we study at school. Our everyday human experience is also education. We need a language to share human experiences with each other. Therefore, education and language are connected.

Every society uses a language for exchanging information in daily life. Thus, language and life are inseparably intertwined. Since education is also informational exchange, education and language should be intertwined the same way.

Language, education, and life are intimately connected with each other.

3.1 Language as the basis of education

To acquire knowledge through education, students should have language skills. They need listening skills to understand what the teacher is saying, reading skills to read books, speaking skills to express their ideas, and writing skills to describe their thoughts. Hence, what we call language skills consists of listening, reading, speaking, and writing skills. Elementary education should train students in these skills. It forms the basis for higher education.

However, since the objective in current educational systems is to write examinations to get grades, students do not acquire any skills except writing. They do not have the courage to express themselves in front of scholars. They do not have the habit of reading good books. Their writing is not of a good standard. There is a notion among teachers that if students get the right answers, they can get full credit even if there are grammatical errors. Under these conditions, where is the incentive for students to get language skills? Even teachers do not have these skills, because this practice had started when they were students.

The language a society uses in its everyday life is called the native language of that society. In general, it is easy to see which language is in use in a region. When we go to the store and buy things which language do we speak?

When we travel by bus which language do we speak with the conductor and fellow passengers? Which language do the teachers and students talk at school and outside the classroom? That is the native language of that region.

If education should be connected to life, it should naturally be in this language. Even in offices that operate in English, staff members talk in this language among themselves! Doesn't it look artificial if education and information exchange in offices are in a foreign language? Shouldn't we change such a situation? Shouldn't we at least think about how to change it?

In Tamilnadu higher education is only available in English. Even for elementary education, people of economically upper class and middle class tend to send their children to private schools emphasizing English. Mostly people of economically lower class send their children to government schools. Although there is Tamil medium education in government schools, even these schools are converting to English medium. There are English words and English style in textbooks for Tamil medium education too. Thus, education in Tamilnadu is getting converted to English *in toto*.

The medium of education changing from native language to a foreign language is dangerous. Please understand that I am not saying this because of my love for Tamil. I am not going to say that your children should not learn English, or they should only study in Tamil. We will come back to such practical questions later. All I need now is to trigger your thinking. If you understood what I have said so far, this conclusion arises by itself.

When education is in a foreign language, it stands separated from life. Society does not benefit from education. Science, technology, and medicine appear to be imported from abroad. In fact, they are common to all people of the world. They are based on discoveries about nature. All people of earth should benefit from them. All people of the world can contribute to them.

I said in the introduction that society operates at several levels. Tamil is the language for Tamil society. Indian unity is a concept for Indian society. But science and technology are for the world society.

An important reason for Indian education seeming to bring us foreign concepts is that it is in a foreign language. Because of this, we do not use what we learn in school at home. Let us see an example.

We all study at ninth or tenth standard in science class about nutrients and their role in health. We study about balanced diet too. But do we use that knowledge in our lives? We eat rice or dosa just like our grandparents showed us. This results in an excess of carbohydrates in our body and causes diseases like diabetes. Likewise, we do not bring home the importance of physical exercise.

Under these circumstances, how can we expect people to bring home what they have learned at school to solve life problems and social problems? Will they engage in research to create the products and services needed for society? Current education does not offer such an ability to think. Your children receiving such education join foreign companies as servants. Foreigners research and invent. They make products using your children and sell them to you.

A simple way of destroying a society is to separate its native language from its education. Then education separates from life too.

3.2 Multilingual policy

India is a country where many kinds of people live. It is a diverse country rich in arts and culture. There are people of many religions. They speak many languages. The English gathered what was many countries earlier and left it as one on independence. The scholars who separated the country into many states at that time did it based on language, because they knew that language is more fundamental than art, religion, and culture; and it is more intimately related to life.

Now, the question arises as to how people of different states speaking different languages can communicate among themselves. Is not a common language needed for this? We said that education is the exchange of knowledge among societies. Then, for example, how can the Tamil society exchange knowledge with other societies? In which language? Don't you need a connection language for this?

Definitely! For Tamilnadu it may be Hindi or English. For argument's sake, let us say that it is English. But everyone in Tamilnadu does not need to learn English. If a society needs education from another society, a small group from the first society should learn the language of the second society and bring the wealth of knowledge to the native language. This is the simple solution that would occur to anyone with straight thinking. Is it fair to require that everyone in a society should learn the language of another society? Moreover, if all Tamil people must learn English to get the knowledge from America, shouldn't everyone learn Chinese to get China's knowledge? Shouldn't they learn Japanese to get Japan's? The straightforward solution is that a team of people who know Tamil and English should present the American knowledge to Tamils; another team of experts in Tamil and Chinese should bring the knowledge from China; yet another from Japan. This way Tamils can get knowledge from all societies and export their knowledge to others.

Those who say that English should be the language of education in Tamilnadu would argue that English is the language of the world. This is completely wrong (Pennycock 2017). English is the native language in England, USA, and Australia. In no other country it is mandated that higher education for everyone should be in English. Some countries teach English as a subject in high school. But, as far as I know, not having higher education in native language and even elementary education being converted to English is only happening in India.

In India there is trilingual policy. Tamilnadu had rejected Hindi and adopted a bilingual policy. If Hindi is a foreign language, isn't English more so? Why do those who hate Hindi and Sanskrit roll out the red carpet for English? This is based on the wrong concept that English is the language of the world.

In Tamilnadu even this bilingual policy is not functioning properly. We would expect Tamils to be conversant both in Tamil and in English. But the fact is that they are not conversant in any of them. When those Tamils who think that they know English go to English speaking countries, they realize that they do not know English well.

This is what I realized. The Indian Institute of Technology at Chennai (IIT, Madras) is considered one of the best for higher education in India. Mostly students from upper class families who studied in the top English medium private schools come here to study. As an exception I studied there too for my postgraduate. Thinking that I knew English well because of my studying there, I went to America for my doctoral study in 1978. After going there, I understood that I did not know English. I could not understand what the people there were saying, and they could not understand me. But, about a year later, I understood and spoke English well.

What we can gather from this is that the best way to learn a language is to be immersed in a society that speaks that language. In India nobody is immersed in a society that speaks English. Language skills are acquired by habit. Then why can't Tamils habituate in English? Because they are immersed in a Tamil speaking society. Even your teachers do not know English well. Even if you get hundred percent in the exams they conduct, you do not know English well. Because the teachers are also immersed in a Tamil society. To them too, Tamil is the native language and English is a foreign language.

English is a language that is very different from Tamil. There are many fundamental differences between Tamil and English. Due to these differences, it is as difficult for a Tamil person to learn English as it is for an Englishperson to learn Tamil. Tamil natives while attempting to get foreign language skills fail in their native language as well.

Language is the basis for education. People should know how to speak, read, and write in any one language. Language skills are a prerequisite for studying other subjects such as mathematics, science, technology, and arts. Bilingual education is neither here nor there. Students do not have skills in Tamil; they do not have skills in English. They speak a language that is a mixture of the two. This mixed language is not suitable for higher education and for higher thinking. Because of this, most of them continue to do what they are told without thinking.

Since Hindi was imposed from outside Tamilnadu, Tamils rejected it. But they have imposed English on themselves. This makes it easy for the English-speaking countries to utilize even the small human resource of Tamilnadu that is successful in education. Not only that; it prevents most of Tamils from getting a quality education.

At this point, you may understand how important it is to train children in their native language.

3.3 Language in employment

The true meaning of being educated is being knowledgeable. But in Tamilnadu there is a misconception that those who know English are educated and therefore employment opportunities are for those who know English. This separates their native language first from education and then from life.

There is a widespread notion in Tamilnadu that learning in English is more respectable and schools that teach in English provide superior education. Because of this, those who study in English medium get most employment opportunities. Even those in jobs where English is not needed, particularly where Tamil is needed, do not know Tamil. I am not just saying that they mix English words when they speak. I am saying that they have not formally learned Tamil and they do not know Tamil grammar.

When you listen to announcements and talks on radio, television, and movies meant for Tamil people, it becomes clear that they have not been trained in speaking.

They speak a crass language in the name of colloquial Tamil. They do not know how to say precisely and concisely what they want to say. They have plenty of opportunity to write down what they need to say, practice, and then speak; or at least rehearse in their minds just a few minutes before speaking. They do not make use of such opportunities. After living in Tamilnadu for a few years, I returned to the United States. In a cooking show I saw on television, the woman goes about her cooking activities while at the same time describing her actions very clearly in beautiful and correct English. I was ashamed that we couldn't talk like that in Tamil. American education has prepared them to talk like that. Indian education has not provided such training.

Very bad grammatical mistakes and lack of clarity abound in dailies and magazines published in Tamil. Why haven't the schools that prepare students well for jobs in foreign corporations prepared them for these jobs? Why haven't they trained them for speaking and writing in good Tamil?

Once I asked a boy studying in an English medium school why Tamils should know English. He replied, "Tamil is my mother tongue. I know it. I don't know English. That is why I am studying it". By this logic, no one in America should study English in school; they should study Tamil which they do not know. They should learn all subjects in Tamil. But in fact, all students in America study English grammar and literature well and acquire the listening, reading, speaking, and writing skills I mentioned above in elementary school and improve them in high school. Based on such language skills they receive higher education and conduct top class research. The computers, cell phones, televisions, washing machines, and dishwashers that are selling in India today were designed by the American people with such research.

Another time, a daughter of my relative asked me to write an application in English for a job as a Tamil teacher she was applying. I told her to write a first draft as best as she could and offered to help by correcting and improving it. She refused. The reason is that she can't write a line in

English. Well, that is ok, I said. For a position as Tamil teacher, why couldn't she write in Tamil, I asked stupidly. Surprised, she said, "But writing in English is prestigious, uncle!". For a Tamil teacher job, it is prestigious to apply in English even by getting someone else to write it.

On the one hand, they say you won't get a job if you study in Tamil medium. On the other hand, where Tamil is needed, they don't employ people who know Tamil. Are not Tamil scholars needed in places such as television, radio, newspaper, magazine, publishing houses of Tamilnadu? How can there not be jobs if you study in Tamil? Tamil people need numerous services. Don't you need knowledge of Tamil to provide these services? Why should someone born and brought up in Tamilnadu wanting to provide medical services to Tamil people study medicine in English? Why should someone born and brought up in Tamilnadu wanting to provide legal services to Tamil people study law in English? The reason is that the teachers who teach these professions do not know Tamil. They would say as an excuse that the required textbooks are not available in Tamil. If they aren't, whose responsibility is it to make them? Is it not the responsibility of these educators? Is it not the responsibility of the government officials who make educational policies? What is the meaning of them abdicating such responsibility? It means that they do not care about Tamil people. Just like creating social strata with castes in the old days, now they are creating it with language. Children from families which know English are considered high and children from Tamil families are considered low.

3.4 Language and society

When I live in India, I withdraw money from ATM. Then someone would extend their ATM card and ask me to get money for them. Some of these people may be illiterate. Some others may not know how to operate the ATM because its interface is in English. Neither is good for society. All members of a society should receive basic education.

Education and services should be in people's native language.

When services are provided in a foreign language, they do not reach the people. People cannot understand the events in their society. People understanding social affairs is part of education. Education is something that continues for life.

If anyone talks about the law in Tamilnadu, people sneer at them. Law stands apart from people's lives. The laws in the lawbooks are different from the rules people follow by themselves. This is obvious when we look at the rules that drivers follow when they drive. People do not understand the way courts work in English. How many law experts are there in Tamilnadu? It didn't occur to any of the honorable judges, attorneys, lawyers, and advisors to write the law in Tamil! Why? They do not care about people. They say as an excuse that Tamil is not a suitable language for describing law. The fact is that they do not know Tamil. They may not admit it. Perhaps they think of themselves as great scholars and the people's language of Tamil is beneath them. They should be ashamed to call themselves legal experts. What difference does make if the law not useful to people is alive or dead?

As far as I have seen in India, even people who have had college education do not have a basic knowledge of human anatomy. There is a widespread notion that modern medicine is foreign medicine, and the local medicine is superior. The fact is that something like what Indians call local medicine existed everywhere in the world at some point in history. Modern medicine has gradually evolved from it and that is what we now call English medicine in India. Since we study modern medicine in English, we see it as English medicine.

Since services such as banking, law, medicine, science are not in people's language, people stand apart from them. They do not see these services as meant for them. If upper-class people want to keep the public away from services, offering the services in a language known only to them instead of people's language is a great way. Earlier brahmins were doing this in Sanskrit. Now the 'educated' of all castes are doing it in English.

3.5 The English glamor

Since education is in English and those who know English are considered upper-class, even those who do not know English and those who know a little bit of English want to show themselves as knowing English. Because of this, people do not have genuine skills in either Tamil or English. Without language skills, the learning capacity of society is very low.

Because of English glamor, youngsters consider low of speaking and writing in Tamil. Education should change such trends. Teachers should learn Tamil well and should practice it with students. Teachers should be pioneers and set examples for removing the glamor of English. A situation should arise where students should be proud of being able to speak and write in good Tamil. Only when such a time arrives, education will improve.

Upper-class people pay tens of thousands of rupees to buy cell phones, computers, televisions, washing machines or other such things from foreign countries. But if the local milk vendor wants to raise the price of milk by five rupees per liter, they do not like it. They think that the milk vendor is robbing them. Is this not an insult to the milk vendor?

4 Education as commodity

4.1 Government responsibility

Education is not only the transfer of knowledge from parents to children. We saw in section 2.8 that it also transfers knowledge among different parts of society. Then, just like digging a well for the benefit of the whole town, education is also a social activity. With the aim of advancing society, all children of society should be educated, and everyone should contribute according to their ability to their own benefit and to the benefit of society at every level. Thus, acquiring knowledge is the **right** of all children, and using the gained knowledge to contribute to society is the **responsibility** of all adults.

Society operates at local level, state level, country level, and world level. Education in a society, in addition to transferring knowledge of that society, should receive from other societies as needed and present to its people. From social values, the unethical should be avoided and the ethical should be taught. Teachers, education officials, and government officials who develop educational policies at state level and central level should follow these principles for social benefits.

People elect representatives to the government for performing social activities at state and national levels. Education is a social activity and an important responsibility of the government.

Education is considered a fundamental human right all over the world. Many countries have enacted regulations to provide free education to all children without economic differentiation. In India we should consider not only economic differences, but also differences due to caste, religion, domicile, etc.

To provide education to all children of India without such differences, the eighty sixth amendment called the Right to Education (RTE) Act was inserted into the constitution in 2002. This act is sometimes referred to as "free and compulsory education". But we should understand the meaning of compulsory education correctly.

This act does not make it compulsory for all children to go to school. It says that the governments should compulsorily provide education to any child of India who desires it. The compulsion is on governments, not on children or parents. Education cannot be denied based on caste or domicile. This government education should be free.

If parents desire, they can provide their children with a different kind of education. For example, they can spend money for a private school; parents can educate their children at home. But, for those who cannot or do not want to do so, there must be free government schools at all places where everyone can send their children. This facility should be available to everyone including mountain tribes, forest tribes, nomadic tribes, scheduled castes, and beggars. This is the implication of the act.

4.2 Privatization

So says the law. But what happens in practice?

Year	2014-15	2015-16	2016-17
Enrolment in government schools (1-12)	144 194 283	143 152 245	137 222 799
Enrolment in private schools (1-12)	79 991 560	82 421 710	80 582 804
Difference in enrolment	64 202 723	60 730 535	56 639 995
Private percent	35.7%	36.5%	37.0%

The data provided by a report of Rajya Sabha session 246 (2018) show, as shown in the table, that the enrollment in private school tends to increase. Many other reports also show increasing enrollment in private schools and at the same time declining enrollment in public schools. Since we see this in practice, I do not list such statistics. All these data show that in the last few decades private schools have been attracting students rapidly. It seems that this trend will continue till private schools fully engulf the enrollment completely.

The direction is reversed in progressive countries. There, 84% of students attend public schools, 12% go to government sponsored private schools, and 4% go to independent private schools (OECD 2016).

Despite being equal rights for people, education is becoming private property in India. Private schools are reachable only for children from well-to-do families. But even less well-to-do families sacrifice other needs and use up remaining belongings to send their children to private schools. Only the poor people who cannot even do that send children to public schools.

While there is a law mandating the government to provide free education to all children, why do people not use that service and are attracted to private schools? There may be many reasons for it. Let us consider them one by one.

One reason is a widespread notion that children who study in private schools through English have better job opportunities. Even if this were true, we should try to change it rather than fall prey to it. Wherever they study, students study the same subjects. Children with intelligence and inspiration will study well and advance. Another reason may be that studying in English helps to go abroad. This is not true. Knowing English as a language may be helpful in countries speaking English. But it is not necessary to study all subjects in English.

Some parents say that public schools lack facilities and safety, and that teachers do not pay attention to their children. We should try to change this too, and not make it worse. If the government does not do its job well, we should think of ways to question the government. Let us not forget that it is in people's hands to elect governments.

Some seem to fear that children of the poor and the lowered castes study in public schools and these children will spoil their children by association. How much confidence these people have in their children! Why can't the other children be 'redeemed' by associating with their children? It is antisocial to consider our children as good and other children as bad. The 'other' children subjected to such division would grow up with hatred. It creates an antisocial population. One day when your child is an adult, if he or she are in a road accident, the 'other' person would run away with jewelry. Is this the kind of society you want to leave your children to live in?

India is a diverse country with people of different language, culture, arts, habits, etc. We can proudly celebrate this diversity, or we can use it for division. These are natural differences among people. But caste creates social stratification artificially in people. Since this does not arise from people's natural attributes and created by people, this is artificial. In principle, religion does not create stratification; but it also creates an artificial division among people. Most people use differences in economic status, domicile (rural versus urban), and occupation as causes for social stratification. We may appreciate differences. Curiosity about different people is enjoyable. But stratification is antisocial. It creates xenophobic societies.

The objective of education is to make a cohesive society. Private education yields the opposite effect. The net result of private education is to separate children of well-to-do families and impart a feeling of superiority to them, and a feeling of inferiority to those who cannot afford to go to such schools.

I am not saying this to make you transfer your child from private school to public school today. My aim is to induce your thinking. First, we need to create awareness in society. Accepting these ideas in principle is a first step. Then there is a chance for gradual change.

4.3 Comparing outcomes

Whether learning outcome is better or worse in private schools than public schools is a question asked not only in India but also in many countries such as the USA. In India the public opinion is clearly in favor of private schools. But there is no basis for this feeling. Many research reports

(Desai 2008) reveal that there is no significant difference in learning outcomes between these types of schools.

Parents who send their children to private schools happen to be wealthy and educated. Since they value education highly, they encourage children to work hard in studying well and help with homework. If there is an improvement in the learning of private school students, it may be due to parents' inducement and not by the quality of education. Students' scores in competitive examinations are directly related to parents' educational qualifications, urban living, household income, and standard of living.

The difference between private and public schools varies among states. In states like Bihar, Uttar Pradesh, Uttarakhand, and Madya Pradesh, private education is a little better than public education. Generally, public enterprises perform poorly in these states. It is noted that these are India's poor states. In states like Haryana and Tamilnadu, enrollment in private schools is higher but public-school students are more skillful.

Thus, the assumption that private schools in India are superior becomes false. Although private school students fare better nationally, it is due to the educational level of parents. In states like Tamilnadu public schools are better.

We saw the difference between the two kinds of schools within India and among states. But let us see where India is in relation to the countries in the world. In an assessment called Program for International Student Assessment (PISA) in 2009 India came at 72nd position out of 74 countries. Shameful! After 2009 India did not participate in that assessment.

Indian students are very low in reading and arithmetic. When private and public schools are on the same boat, the question of who is better is meaningless.

4.4 Private education as commercial

What is the objective of private schools? Profit oriented businesspersons are running private schools. We saw that the objective of education is to provide knowledge to children. But the objective of private schools is to make money. They earn money by creating differences and division among people. They exploit the wrong ideas prevailing in people that English education is better and government schools are of low quality. They manure and grow such ideas. Parents and employers succumb to this illusion.

Not studying in Tamil or studying in English does not make children knowledgeable. They study the same subjects at any school in any language. Studying in a foreign language is harder, not easier. Intelligent students can acquire knowledge in any way. While studying in their native languages, more students can more easily become scholars.

Educating not only the rich but all children of society and selecting skillful students from all sections of society for employment is good for corporations. But if that is done, private schools will not have income, and the rich people would not like it.

The education that was intimately connected with society in the past is now a separate entity removed from society. It has lost its original objective and is now sold to the rich.

When I was in college in the 1970s, private education and English medium education were exceptions. Those days a few famous schools in cities collected fees from parents and provided quality education through English. Those who studied here were wealthy, not necessarily intelligent. Someone who studied in such a school was my classmate in college. He wanted to copy from me during examinations. Since there was English glamor in cities even then, private school graduates were held higher than public school graduates. And there was stiff competition to enroll in such schools.

As years went on, business-oriented entrepreneurs started many more English medium schools to exploit the competition. These were not of high quality as the originals. Just like the turkey emulating a dancing peacock (கான

மயிலாடக் கண்டிருந்த வான்கோழி), middle class parents trying to emulate upper class enrolled their children in these schools. Those who started these schools became rich. Other businesspersons who saw this business opportunity with small investment and huge returns started more such schools. Quality diminished further. Expanding thus, English medium schools arrived at small towns. Villagers assuming that city people are smart and wanting to emulate them, are now bussing their children to these schools in nearby towns. This is the story of the evolution and proliferation of private schools. In this story there is no thought about social needs, the meaning of education, or how to educate the future citizens of society.

Private education, in particular college education and professional education, is a commodity highly in demand and highly profitable. It has exponential return on investment unimaginable in any other profession. Curriculum and syllabus are geared toward gratifying capitalistic interests. They do not address the broad needs of society.

In India private education is mostly a family business. Teaching and other services are not carried out in accordance with any educational philosophy, but in accordance with the desires of the managing family. Though there may be some exceptions, this is the widespread trend all over India. In other countries we find the opposite. Famous universities such as Oxford, Cambridge, Harvard, Stanford, and Princeton are all private universities. In these institutions, private directors handle education consistent with broad social needs.

In a society where private players do not have such interests, the government should handle education directly, because a government can operate without prejudice, differentiation, or attachment. It can establish equality in creating and propagating knowledge. It can level any existing inequality. But the current and recent governments at the center and in states of India have failed in this responsibility. They have left education to profit-oriented businesses. It is not surprising that these businesses provide the wealthy with an education suitable and needed for them. As a total result, Indian society, having forgotten the true objectives of education, is moving towards an uncivilized state.

The constitution says that private education should be a nonprofit charitable activity. That is, those who run it can only get teachers' salary and other expenses from students as fees. Any excess funds can only be spent to develop the schools. There should not be any net profit, the law says. But educational institutions have devised methods to overcome these requirements.

For this, they have created a two-level structure. A charity runs the school. It is accounted as a nonprofit organization. The school property belongs to another organization which leases the building to the school and provides services such as management and technology. The school pays rent and fees to the other organization. After teacher salaries and other small expenses, the rest of the funds flows to this organization in the name of rent and fees. Since this is a profit-oriented business, its owners can take its income.

Many management aspects are involved in running a school such as admission, collecting fees, financial management, employment, accounting, purchasing, logistics, transportation, and facility management. Most private schools do not follow sound management principles. They do not want to spend money appointing qualified managers. These educational institutions operate as a family business like a retail store. Each family member takes an activity under their control. They do not give teachers the flexibility to improve education. The head of the family becomes the uncrowned king of education. No law or regulation can control them. They know all manipulations and fabrications. They show in the books that all requirements of the law are satisfied.

Businesspersons control education, not educators or scholars. It is natural in a profit-oriented business to reduce expenses and increase income as much as possible. Isn't it good business practice to appoint less qualified teachers at lower salaries to reduce expenses? You can imagine the resulting quality of education.

4.5 GATS of WTO

GATS and WTO are not letters I have typed randomly on the keyboard. They stand for General Agreement on Trade in Services and World Trade Organization respectively. WTO regulates trade among participating countries and creates the rules and agreements for it. One of its agreements is GATS. This agreement describes trade rules for common use by countries participating in WTO and liberalizes commerce. India is one of the 164 participating countries. Every country can choose which services to liberalize from a list.

Services regulated by GATS include computer related services, research and development, real estate, leases, communication, construction, and distribution. In 1996 educational services were added. Teams of scholars from many countries including Canada, USA, and Europe opposed it (Sath 2006) saying that including educational services as commercial services is wrong. Indian governments did not take such objections into account and embraced GATS.

Higher education is a public service. It is not a saleable product. Hence, it should be under the direct supervision of the respective governments. If educational services are exported from developed countries to developing countries, it should be assured to augment the local educational system and not replace it, the experts opine. Indian governments did not heed this advice either.

WTO is clearly commercially oriented. In the last section we saw that Indian businesspersons want to dominate education. This happens worldwide. That is, businesspeople all over the world want to make money by selling education. But the governments and respectable universities in developed countries oppose this trend and protect education. In India governments and educational institutions fall in line with WTO-GATS.

Commerce, communication, and other activities are becoming globalized. We cannot avoid education becoming global too. But it should be done based on social needs in the country. Instead, it is done according to the commercial interests in developed countries. The English glamor and foreign glamor in Indian people facilitate it.

According to the GATS policy, there are four commercial modes in every service. In education they are (1) getting education by paying fees to foreign entities (2) going abroad to get education, (3) foreign entities establishing branches to offer education, and (4) foreign teachers visiting to educate.

Since these four modes are reciprocal between countries, they seem on the surface to be aspects of globalization. But in practice, consider how many Indian students want to study in America and how many American students want to study in India. Clearly, education along with language and culture are imported from developed countries to developing countries.

According to GATS foreign universities can set up their campuses in India. This too appears to be beneficial to India when viewed superficially. But educational institutions offer poor services in their foreign campuses because their objective is commercial only. The quality of education, curriculum, research, and infrastructure found in their home campuses are controlled by the governments and scholars there. There is no such quality control in the international campuses of these universities. High quality institutions do not like to establish foreign campuses because it is hard to maintain quality and their reputation.

Since it is expensive to buy education from abroad, only the upper class in India benefit from this. These foreign services do not reach the middle class and lower class. Because of this, the upper class are converting to western cultures and poor people get further separated from education.

4.6 The future

If this privatization trend continues, it will be complete sometime in the future. Education will be completely commercial, and governments will give up running public schools. Then education for the benefit of people will not exist even nominally. The poor will not get any education. As usual governments will allow the private sector to reign supreme without any control. Educational institutions will determine student fees. Governments will lose the ability to redesign teacher employment, salary, student admission, etc. for the benefit of society.

People expect that private education provides quality education. This is an illusion. They do not distinguish between English education and quality education. The middle class expects to elevate their children to upper class by sending them to private schools. But there is no space in the upper class for everybody. Lower class people expect to elevate their children to middle class by sending them to at least government school. The government schools are not fulfilling it. Even the education the upper class is getting is not great in the international setting.

A few students here and there can study "well" and elevate their social status. But the upper class is interested in keeping other classes from mixing with them. They will design education accordingly. Rulers, officials, and educators will modify education such that even the here and there elevation does not occur. Even now, most of the upper class get educated and employed well to keep their upper-class status. But the number of people elevated from middle class and lower class is very small. They are the exceptions.

Those who are middle class now, since they get pseudo education, will become poor. Even if they study in English, they cannot compote in education and employment with the upper class. The policies of the central and state governments of India will continue to be favorable to the upper class. Agreements like WTO-GATS unite the upper class of the world through commerce. Since the middle class and lower class do not have the money the WTO members need, GATS neglects them.

What is the net result of globalization? The upper class in all countries will be united by using one language (English) and adopt one culture (western). All others will be neglected, will suffer in poverty for a long time, and finally perish. Then a new world will arise. And then they will all live happily ever after.

5 Education and politics

We saw in section 4.1 that it is the government's responsibility to provide education to everyone in the country. In section 3.1 we saw that education in the native language is most effective in imparting knowledge to people. We saw in section 4.3 that private education does not provide quality education and in section 4.4 that it provides employment opportunities only to the upper class. From all this we can conclude that the government should phase out private education, provide a quality education to everyone, and encourage them to undertake a profession according to their interests and desires, thereby improving themselves and society. But the governments in India are not doing it. Why?

5.1 Income from private education

We saw in section 4.4 that Indian businesspeople derive good income from private education and in section **Error! Reference source not found.** that foreign businesses benefit from private education in India. Would the politicians keep quite watching these people raking in money? It is only natural that they want a (large) part of that income to go to them!

Except for the very poor, whoever makes money in whatever way, the law provides that the government should take a considerable portion of it as taxes. Businesspeople and the rich have devised numerous ways to escape even that.

Here I am not talking about taxation. Tax goes to the government. I am thinking whether there are ways of taking money to politicians' homes. If there are, they must be occurring under the table secretly, because it is illegal. I do not know if there are such ways. You can guess.

5.2 Economic appearance

Generally, the politicians who oversee the government are interested in making the rules and regulations acceptable to corporate businesses and upper-class people. As mentioned in the previous section, they can also benefit from it. Also, they want to show in the international setting that India is developing fast economically. It is not surprising that they are interested in attributing their development to their being in power and congratulating themselves.

In their view, Indian economy would not improve by educating the poor or elevating their lifestyles. Since the rich have the capital for commerce, they are the ones participating in the country's economic development. Because of this, the rich develop further economically. This is the mechanism of the rich getting richer and the poor getting poorer.

In the world stage India's economy appears to be growing fast. That growth occurs completely in India's upper class. Since this economic growth neglects others, they fall farther behind. The economic polarization of society widens.

The government accepts principles such as WTO-GATES and globalization based on the view that India develops economically when its large businesses develop.

5.3 Social pride

The central government of India likes to uphold the Indian pride and Tamilnadu government the Tamil pride. The central government contaminates education with ancient Hindu principles and Tamilnadu government emphasizes ancient Tamil literature rather than modern language skills. They do not seem to consider what benefits people get from this.

Society operates at many levels as we have seen earlier. Family, relatives, town, caste, language, state, country, and world are different levels of society. If alliance to language, caste, or religion is divisive, then alliance to a country is also a division that separates us from the world, is it not? Indian patriotism is an artificial phenomenon created by the central government of India. Tamilnadu government upholding Tamil pride is also of this nature.

It is natural that people differ by caste, religion, language, country, and culture. There is nothing wrong with differentiating each division. What is wrong is stratification. A hierarchy of superiority and inferiority based on caste is deep rooted in India. It causes several social problems.

All people of the world should appreciate the pride of every country. Everyone should appreciate the pride of every language. In the same way, every caste should be respected by other castes. If the attitude that they are also people like us arises, then there won't be any division. In an equal society there won't be hatred or its consequences.

Creating an attitude to move towards this idealism is the responsibility of education. Setting up such an education is the duty of the government. Electing the politicians to form such a government is the responsibility of the people.

The situation in India today is just opposite. Politicians do not attempt to remove the social stratification created by caste, or differences by religion or language. They appear to scheme how to make use of the differences to their advantage. This causes these differences and consequences to increase.

5.4 Language policy and politics

India is a country where many kinds of people live, people speaking different languages. This is a unique attribute to India not found in any other country of the world. This attribute and the resulting diversity are to be appreciated and celebrated.

At the same time, it causes some problems too. Questions arise such as how people speaking one language can interact with people of other languages, and in which language(s) the central services of the country should be. We can ask the same questions at the international level too. Do we need a world language? If so, what should it be?

The unprejudiced general solution to this problem is that translation services between any two languages should operate among societies to benefit people. Since the day of independence, just as India started building bridges and dams, the central government could have gathered linguists and initiated an infrastructure to provide language services. Just like recovering the bridge expenses through tolls, an arrangement could have been made to collect a small fee when commercial organizations and government departments make use of the services. After the expenses were recovered, the services could have been made available to the public free of charge sponsored by the government. If they had done that, today such a system would have matured, and the country would not have had any language issues. There would have been experts to translate speech and writing between any two languages when and where needed. People would have been highly skilled in their native languages.

Today when computers and artificial intelligence participate in all human endeavors, translation services can be provided by machines. When computer technology developed in other areas, computerizing translation services could have been undertaken. Governments should have encouraged linguists to perform the required research through grants. If that was done, now the cell phones always present in our pockets and handbags when we wander around would have satisfied this need.

None of that happened. What did the governments heretofore do instead? They hung on to the impractical principle that there should be one language for the whole country. This agitated the people. There is no reason to pick any language in the country as the national language. Whichever language was picked, all people speaking other languages would have to learn that language. This would be advantageous to those to whom this language is the native language and a burden to everyone else. Hatred and opposition arising from others is natural.

The central governments of India have acted as if Hindi was the language of India and no other language existed. Hindi is native to Delhi and surrounding areas. The politicians attempting to make this language the Indian language have not understood the true nature of India.

What the central and state governments should have jointly started immediately after independence can be started now. If done so, in a few decades all Indians could be educated in their native languages; intelligent people from all parts of the country can participate in advancing the country instead of only the upper class as it is done today. Then the country will prosper.

5.5 Tests such as NEET

NEET (National Eligibility cum Entrance Test) is an entrance examination conducted nationwide for students who wish to receive medical education. Only a small fraction of students who score high on this test are admitted to medical schools.

Its objective seems noble. It selects those who have the knowledge to become physicians and engages them in medical education. It is good for the country that medical professionals know medicine well. But shouldn't their medical knowledge be tested after they have completed their education?

School education is the responsibility of state governments. SCERT (State Council for Educational Research and Training) in every state designs the curriculum and syllabus based on the language, history, culture of the state. NCERT (National Council for Educational Research and Training) designs a nationwide curriculum. The central curriculum is followed in Central Schools managed by CBSE (Central Board of Secondary Education). These schools were created for the children of central government employees.

NEET is based on the national curriculum devised by NCERT. Hence, by design it is advantageous to the central government employees. They are military officers, professors at central universities like IITs, the IAS (Indian Administrative Services) and IPS (Indian Police Service) officers of the central government and other officials.

The central government has created a school system for the upper-class children to study and an entrance test called NEET so that only those who studied in these schools can get admission to medical colleges.

But, what about the upper-class people who are not central government employees? They send their children to special expensive private schools created just for the purpose of training and preparing for NEET. The poor do not even know the details of NEET or how children can prepare for it. Even if they know, they do not have the monetary means.

The IITs (Indian Institutes of Technology) and IISc (Indian Institute of Science) considered the top higher educational institutions in the country by the upper class also have similar tests. One of them is JEE (Joint Entrance Examination). This means that all higher education is for the economic upper class. Poor and lowered caste children of society succeeding in these tests is an exception. There are very few.

Evaluating students by these and other tests is mechanical. It is questionable whether they evaluate students' real intelligence or knowledge. The grader of these tests is not the one who taught the student. They are somewhere else. They do not know anything about this student. Students can only manifest their skills through the bottleneck of written answers to questions. How they view and analyze a problem, approach the solution, whether they think deeply, and how they describe their ideas in words (by writing and speaking) are not considered by this evaluation method.

Consider the following question. Murugan has eaten half of his pizza. Ahmed has eaten one third of his pizza. Is it correct to say that Ahmed has eaten more pizza than Murugan? Explain.

The answer given in the answer key for grading is: *No, because one third is less than half.*

A student's answer: *Yes, when Ahmed's pizza is larger than Murugan's by a factor of more than one and half.*

Since the phrase "of the same size" is not present in the question the student considered all situations. We should appreciate this student as a good thinker. But our education system gives them a zero.

5.6 What is good for elections?

In a democratic country, electing the government is the people's responsibility. In India the constitution grants voting right to everyone 18 years of age or older. For the people to utilize this right properly and elect a suitable government, they should have a good understanding of the political system of the country, the structure of the government, the process of electing representatives, and its consequences. When they cast their votes without such understanding, society may not elect a government that is suitable for them.

Now, consider a society of uneducated people. Politicians can easily handle them. They can exploit people's misconceptions, talk accordingly, and induce them to vote for them. In this case, how does the elected government function? Will it fulfil its responsibilities of educating people? If people become knowledgeable, then what kind of government will they elect? They can elect a different government that can be beneficial to society, can't they? Therefore, it is to the politicians' advantage to keep people ignorant.

Thus, the government elected by uneducated people will keep the population uneducated with the aim of winning the next election. I am not talking about any one party. They are all in the same basket.

6 Education and dominance

Let us see two examples of how people can use education in their favor when they want to hold power in their hands and rule as dictators according to their wishes. These dictators glorify their own kind of people and oppress others. Patriotism and national pride are the magical words they use.

In Germany there was a dictator called Adolf Hitler. History notes his rule as fascism. Fascism is based on a fanatical liking for people like oneself and a loathing for other kinds of people. A dictator using their authority and military power to uphold such fanaticism and loathing as well as to quash opposition is an aspect of fascism. Racial purity and Germanic pride are special features of Hitler's fascism.

At about the same period Benito Mussolini was a dictator in Italy.

To understand how dictators like Hitler and Mussolini operate, we first need to understand the concepts of nation, state, and country.

6.1 Nation, State, and Country

Now we need to distinguish between nation and country. In common usage we interchange the terms as if they have the same meaning. But political science uses the terms for two different concepts. We will also see a related term called state.

A **Nation** represents a group of people with a common attribute such as religion, language, habits, or culture. When the people of a region devise a method of government and live as a society, it is called a **State**. Many states can join to form a **Federal State**. A state without any subdivision is called a **Unitary State**. At present the world is not a single State. The part of the earth where people live is divided into many countries. A **Country** may be a single state or a federal state.

People of a nation need not be organized as a state. If they are, it is called a **Nation State**. For example, the collection of Tamils all over the world can be called the Tamil Nation. But there is no Tamil State. Why can't Tamilnadu be called a Tamil State? Because, Tamils live in other parts of the world too, and other people can live in Tamilnadu. Even though most states of India are structured based on languages, they are not nation states.

The country we generally call America, the United States of America (USA) is a federal state consisting of 50 states and some territories. India is a federal state consisting of 28 states and 8 union territories.

After distinguishing between nation and state, we should realize that in daily life we interchange these terms. What we call national anthem is really the song for the state (country) called India. It would have been more appropriate to call it the country anthem.

6.2 Fascistic rule

After understanding the difference between nation and state, let us return to the motivation of fascism. *Fascistic rule tries to convert a county where different kinds of people live into a nation state for a particular kind of people.* Fascistic rule and the resulting nation state arise on the basis that the culture of a nation is superior to all others and its advance more important. An individual takes pride in belonging to a nation is the nationalistic principle. This nation can be based on a caste, religion, language, race, or belief.

Whose caste, religion, language, race, or belief would it be? It would be the high caste, majority religion or language, dominating race or belief. Such a national government can not only neglect the values, cultural traditions, and rights of the oppressed castes, minority religions, etc., but also try to destroy them. That is what happened in Hitler's Germany.

Hitler tried to make Germany a country for Aryans. He oppressed others with his autocracy and military power. He tried to create in Aryans the pride that they are superior.

Mussolini considered every member of society connected to other members as well as the history and culture of the society, and that the unified mind of a society manifests through its citizens. He tried to make everyone follow what he considered Italy's mind. He expected people to realize the pride of the Roman Empire and to work for the country with patriotism.

These attempts appeared to be successful for a time and then failed.

6.3 Education as a tool of fascism

Hitler and Mussolini used education to instill fascistic principles in children at young ages. Both had understood that education can be effectively used as a tool to make a country a nation state of a particular kind of people.

The education they offered did not sharpen children's intelligence or make them thinkers. Without thinking, they just listened to what teachers said about national pride and patriotism. The education that imposes the national principles of a particular people is called a national education.

Hitler said, "no boy or girl ... leave school without having led to an ultimate realization of the necessity and essence of blood purity". Racial struggle, German pride, rewritten German history, and social theories dominated education. The curriculum was adjusted to the needs of the national government. Science lessons included principles of shooting, military aviation, building bridges, and the effects of poisonous gases.

Mussolini followed Hitler and tried a fascistic nationalism in Italy. During his rule, Giovanni Gentile reformed education. The principle that the mind of a society manifests through the people formed the basis of education in all private and public schools from nursery schools to universities. Educational institutions were given the responsibility of seeding national cultural values such as virility, heroism, and patriotism in students. A law enacted in December 1925 removed numerous teachers who did not embrace fascistic principles. The gradual centralization of education was completed when the Ministry of National Education was created. National textbooks consistent with fascistic ideals became compulsory.

6.4 Fascism in Indian education

It is a historical fact that national governments have the tradition of using education as a tool for inculcating national principles. Nationalism is a forced morale and attitude based on the views of a dominant social group. Education by national governments have always maintained the benefits of dominant groups as principal curricula.

This is why they have developed an educational system of memorizing what they are told without thinking or questioning. If people depressed socially and economically receive enough education to think, wouldn't they raise questions on the *status quo* and try to rise beyond the bounds? This is why dominant authorities create an obedient education method from top to bottom that blunts students' intelligence. This not only deprives people of true education but feeds the doctrines of the dominant in the name of education.

There are such aspects in the education currently in India. New educational policies enhance these aspects further. These policies hide India's diversity and glorifies a nation called India, high caste Hindus, and Hindi as a single language. The magical incantation of the current Indian government is One nation, One language, One religion, One caste, One tax, One educational policy.

Indian education glorifying Indian pride is equivalent to Hitler glorifying Germanic pride and Mussolini Italian pride. These are not the true prides of the counties. To place themselves as higher class and dominate over others, they inculcate their pride as national pride through education. The true pride of India is its diversity. Indian education does not breath a word of it.

Unity in Diversity should be the magical incantation of India. Although many kinds of people live in India, they respect each other and live in peace should be the desired situation. Education should create such a situation. Instead, current education has created a situation where one among the many kinds of people dominate, and neglect and suppress other castes, religion, poor, rural residents, etc.

7 National educational policy

The current education system in India is based on a document titled "National Education Policy 2020" released by the Central government. This document is written in English so that only professors and lawyers can understand. Scholars have the responsibility to present the ideas in this document in Tamil (and in other languages) in a way people can understand. Because it affects the future of every child in all nooks and corners of India. For the same reason, every citizen of India has the responsibility to understand the implications of this document and act accordingly.

It is the right of every child in India to get quality school education free of cost and quality higher education at an affordable cost. People of all castes, all religions, all languages should have equal access to education (and everything else), says the Constitution of India. Where there is no equality, the Constitution tries to establish equality by offering relief such as reservations. Such reliefs should prolong until equality is achieved. The new educational policy put forward by the central government proposes no plan to establish such relief measures.

National Educational Policy 2020 (NEP) is a 484-page document in English. In 2019, Jawahar Nesan examined its draft version minutely and published a book describing its shortcomings and their alternatives. I am including many points from that book in various chapters of this book. Professor Nesan has expressed his views after examining this educational policy based on his knowledge obtained by visiting many countries and reading many scholars.

He has done his duty. By bringing this book to you I am doing what I can. What are you going to do to protect the future of your children?

7.1 Indian centric education

NEP says that it proposes an education centered around Indian culture. But we should look carefully at what the authors of this policy refer to as Indian culture. Then it will be clear who would benefit from this and who will be left behind.

India is a country where people of many cultural heritage live, a country with social stratification by caste divisions, a country practicing many religions, a country with regions of different languages. In a country with so much diversity, which can be referred to as the Indian culture? Is it the Tamil culture which gave Thirukkural to the world? Is it the literary tradition in Bengali, Telugu, Marathi? Is it the lifestyle of city dwellers, or simple rural life? Can we proudly refer to the ancient tradition of widow life and burning a wife in the husband's funeral pyre, or the problems modern women face every day for equality? Is it that of the rich people living in multistoried buildings with all facilities, or the poor daily wage earner living near trash dumps? Which one among the followers of many religions such as Saivites, Vaishnavas, Buddhists, Jains, Christians, and Islamists? Can we refer to Brahmin's rituals, or the sufferings of the untouchables? Of the numerous intermediate castes, each has a unique culture, values, and habits. Which one is Indian culture? Is there any such thing called Indian culture which can encompass all these? What are they going to teach as Indian culture?

The answer to this question is in NEP. It recommends that a study of Sanskrit and knowledge about its literature should be presented to students to make them understand Indian pride. It quotes Aryabhata, Chanakya, and Charaka for India's ancient science and intelligence. This would show proudly that ancient India excelled in many arts including music, dance, painting, sculpture, languages, and literature as shown in Kadambari (64 arts), Lalitavistara Sutra (86 arts), Yasodhara's Jayamangala (512), and Bharatha's Natyashastra. It says to include the traditions and morals enriched over thousands of years in India into the curriculum.

In other words, according to NEP, India is made up of the descendants of high caste people of the Veda culture. It is their culture NEP is referring to as Indian culture. People of no other caste, religion, or language have any pride. In the quotes and examples NEP provides there is nothing from other societies of current totality of India. There is no sign of addressing the economic needs of poor people or the social equality of lowered castes. It does not speak of local arts and culture in various regions of India. It is going to teach the pride of the upper caste to all children of India as Indian pride.

In the old days, the epics, fiction, and stories as well as spiritual texts including the Vedas taught to Indian people as Indian morals are full of superstitions. Upper caste people (those who announced themselves to be superior) said these are holy and kept the depressed so that they do not raise questions. This is Indian centric education. This is what NEP wants to continue even today.

Such an education would not change the present social stratification. Instead, it will create contradictions in the minds of children belonging to other societies without this pride. They will find such education irrelevant to their lives. Hence, they will develop a hatred of education and the culture it teaches. Social divisions will widen further.

7.2 Single identity

We know that the central governments are acting on the basis that if India is to be one country it should be a country of one culture, one language, and one identity. We have not forgotten the recent seizure of taxation rights from state governments on the pretext of one tax for one country. States stand begging the center for funds. It is not surprising that the center wants to bring the same condition for education as well. If they have complete authority in education, then the high caste Hindus running the central government can feed their culture and values to students without any hindrance. They can keep people of other castes and religion oppressed.

The central government certainly knows that India is of diverse people. But it denies that fact and tries to impose a particular lifestyle on the people through education. The effect of education on this basis will be upper caste Hindu men dominating over lower castes, other religions, women, the poor, and rural regions. What they call ancient Indian tradition has been doing exactly that.

There is an argument that a single culture, a single identity, and a single language are essential for the unity of India. But that is not true. What is true is that people of all parts of society, all religions, and all languages should work together for the security and economic advances of the country. It is not true that only people of a single religion or single language can cooperate.

Every Indian citizen has two identities. One is Indian, and the other is their state identity. In the state identity the person can be a Marathi, a Bengali, a Malayali, or a Telugu. This is why when India became independent, scholars installed a federal system of government consisting of language-based states. Just as there are men and women among Indians, and there are youngsters and elders among Indians, there are Telugu, Tamil, and Hindi speakers.

In fact, every Indian has a multitude of identities. Just as an object has properties such as appearance, shape, size, color, taste, and smell, a person has many identities such as country, state, caste, religion, and language. Isn't it foolish to say that an object must have only one property? This is what the central government of India has been doing. And the Indian people are silently accepting this foolishness.

If identities such as caste, religion, and language are bad, what is so special about the Indian identity? Why is it superior? Shouldn't we move towards all the people of the world living in harmony? Why are there divisions like Indian, American, Japanese, and Pakistani? Clearly, every person has multiple identities. Indian is their county identity. Tamil is the identity by native language. Hindu is the religious identity. What is wrong is to use these identities for social stratification. Imposing a language or culture on everybody and destroying other languages and cultures is an antisocial activity. Using education as a weapon for this purpose is unforgivable.

There is no other country in the world as diverse as India. People of India differ by language, culture, religious belief, historical richness, etc. Varied people living together as one country is the greatness of India. Unity in Diversity should be the slogan of India. This is the unique attribute to India. This is a unique feature not found in any other country. This is Indian pride. India should celebrate this diversity. Different regions of India excel in different kinds of music, dance, and other arts. True education should appreciate all of these. Choosing one among them and projecting it as Indian culture is an insult to the fundamentals of India.

7.3 The role of states in education

Education for a society should be consistent with the diversity in the society. One education for everybody is not suitable. Every region should receive an education relevant to that region. Everyone should learn the literature of their native language. They should learn the regional arts. Most importantly, it should face the issues and needs of that region.

To facilitate such regional education, in every state there is a council called SCERT (State Council for Educational Research and Training). It designs the curriculum for the schools in that state, publishes textbooks, and conducts examinations.

NEP changes this situation. It introduces concepts such as one curriculum, one textbook, and one examination for the whole country, and puts them to practice. It makes the curriculum and textbooks designed by NCERT (National Council for Educational Research and Training) to be followed nationwide. This makes it easy for the ruling upper caste Hindus to erase the languages and specialties of states and introduce what they consider Indian pride into the textbooks. This is not society-based education. This is dominance-based education.

Developed countries promote decentralized education. For example. USA, like India, was formed as a federation of many states. Here the federal government only outlines the policies to be followed throughout the country. States are responsible for designing curriculum, planning syllabus, evaluating learning outcomes in ways consistent with federal guidelines. Further, there are school districts in many states.

The constitution of India also leaves education to the states. In the seventh schedule of the constitution, there is a list called concurrent list. This lists 47 items in which the central government and state governments take joint responsibility. Education appears on this list. Thus, the constitution says that state governments should participate in education with the central government, rather than having the same education throughout the country. But the central government has directly violated it through NEP. Most of the people in India do not know this, because the central government has implemented it in a hurry without clearly informing the public and without providing sufficient opportunity or time for experts to discuss.

Another scheme the central government implemented quickly without much discussion is the entrance test called NEET (National Eligibility cum Entrance Test) for admissions to medical education. Though this made huge waves throughout the country, it turned upside down a good system that was in place in Tamilnadu until then. Students who were educated in Tamilnadu curriculum suddenly found themselves having to take this test based on the curriculum of the central government. Those who had received high grades in Tamilnadu scored low on NEET and lost the opportunity for medical education.

One of these students is Anita. Her parents belong to a scheduled caste and are poor. In 12th grade, she scored 1176 out of 1200. But on the NEET in 2017, she received 86 out of 720. The testing mode of NEET is different to that extent. She did not get admission even with the reservation for scheduled castes for the medical education commencing in 2018.

After the supreme court of India did not accept the argument by her and others that admission by NEET works against lower caste and poor students, she committed suicide.

Suicides connected with NEET continue even now (Karr 2021). It is high in Tamilnadu.

No one can create a curriculum to reflect the diversely rich cultures and values in India. The central government's attempt to do this is a symptom of a hypocritical nation. A dominant class calling themselves Indian society fantasizes a country of a single identity, a single culture, and a single language. The objective of imposing this fantasy on school children is clear from the motto of NEP. People and scholars should realize its dangerous consequences.

Education should be under the control of scholars, and not politicians.

8 Democratic education

In this chapter, I will describe a method of education suitable for Tamilnadu. This is based on the education system I have seen in the USA and on principles that would benefit students. This can be adapted with small changes to every state in India.

In fact, the education system of the world is outdated in relation to modern lifestyle. It has historically evolved to arrive at the state we see today. What I am going to describe is futuristic. Let us think about how an educational system would be, if we forget the state of education now and design a system based on present technological lifestyle.

It may take several gradual steps to arrive at what I describe starting from the current state. Still, only if we have an ideal target, we will know the direction for our advancement. Otherwise, we will wander aimlessly.

8.1 Prompting to think

We saw that the aim of education should be to prompt students (people) to think, exercise their intelligence, and advance their knowledge.

Education should exercise intelligence so that people can solve issues arising from life. For example, when uneducated poor people need money, they borrow on interest and then suffer. Poor people not being compensated justly for their labor is also a social problem we need to address. But, in general, everyone should know how to live within one's means, and how to provide for unexpected expenses. The skills for setting up a budget for day-to-day living are essential for everyone. If one decides to borrow based on this financial plan, they should do so only after finding answers to questions such as the interest rate, total interest, ability to repay. Education should provide the skills to solve the many problems arising from life.

In other words, education should give us the knowledge needed to conduct our lives well. If getting a job is the aim of education, it will be for the benefit of the employers. It won't be beneficial to us.

The Indian tradition has created and habituated an attitude of considering others smart and following what they say. These others can be higher caste, teachers, or the educated. It is good to listen to scholars. But after listening, we should analyze what we heard with our own intelligence and decide whether to take it or leave it. Only then it becomes our knowledge (Thirukkural 422).

If we do not understand what the teacher says, or it seems wrong to us, we can raise questions. Asking and learning what we don't know does not amount to insulting elders.

We have seen that 'What I say is correct. It is holy. You cannot question it' is the standpoint of dominators and it is fascism. This is the statement by those who want to control society and dominate over it. Social restraint should be what all parts of society jointly follow. It should not be from an autocrat or dominant class.

We say that activities such as horoscope, prayer, and exorcism are based on belief. What is belief? It means that we accept what someone else says without analyzing it in our mind! When we think about each of them, the human mind cannot find any basis for it. Since thinking capacity is low in a society full of superstitions, creativity is also low, along with scientific research, technological advancement, and economic development.

Education should remove people's superstitions and develop thinking skills.

8.2 Technology in education

We are now living in the electronic era. Computers, internet, cell phones are almost in every house, except the very poor. There are many kinds of uses for the cell phones we carry around in our hands. We can listen to music, watch movies, take pictures and videos, play games, send text and audio video to others, and receive them from others. In addition to entertainment, these apps are also used in education and research. Scholars and researchers use it for conferring among ourselves and to share ideas.

Since children are born and brought up with these gadgets, these technologies are natural parts of life to them. How writing on paper is to us, so is using computers or cell phones to them. Under these circumstances, these devices can be used appropriately for enhancing children's knowledge.

Children watch television and play on cell phones before going to school. If there is education in addition to playing on these devices they are very interested in, they would acquire knowledge without getting bored. Educational applications should be designed to not distinguish between play and education. Then education would be a natural extension of play to them. Similarly, children who can read and write can be encouraged to read books they like.

When my parents went to school, they practiced writing on sand. I wrote in school on a slate with chalk sticks. My children practiced with paper and pen. In the future people will only write on computers. Even now paper is becoming obsolete. There was a time when knowledge was conducted through word of mouth. Then they started writing on palm leaves. Palm leaves became obsolete after the advent of paper. Now paper is superseded by electronic media. To go with this trend, paper should be removed from education and all educational material and evaluation methods should be presented electronically. This can only be achieved in phases. But it should be the goal.

When children are introduced to reading and writing, they should be given electronic devices. Governments should provide them to poor children free of charge. These devices may be simple without the full features of a laptop. Students can recognize letters and read simple words in them. At the next level, they should practice typing letters and simple words. They need not practice handwriting. They should practice on Tamil99 keyboards from the beginning. Fine motor skills develop during touch-typing to the same extent as during handwriting. The problem with this is that teachers and those who make educational policies are not used to touch-typing, especially in Tamil. They only teach what their teachers taught them. If so, how can the world advance?

At the next level, skills should be developed in reading, writing, speaking, and numerical calculations using computer and software technologies. Asynchronous learning, learning at student's pace, telelearning, most importantly learning that is interesting to children are possible in digital education.

Software should be developed to guide students in grammar and correct errors. Then teachers can focus on the contents of what students write and give feedback.

Going digital is the trend for the future. It is true that such a system is not in practice anywhere in the world. Why can't Tamilnadu be the pioneer instead of waiting to follow somebody else!

8.3 Unforced education

Students feel that education is imposed on them by the current education system. Once when I was travelling by train, a schoolboy and his parents were my fellow travelers. He was holding a book in English. It was not a textbook, but a story book. After not seeing him open the book for several hours, I said to him, "Buddy, you have a nice book. Won't you read us a story from it?". His face withered. Noticing this, his dad laughed and said, "Just like a grandpa at home pesters you to read, here is another". Then I understood that the boy had not brought the book on his interest, but his grandpa had stuffed it in his hand.

Parents and teachers should orient children to get interested by themselves in reading books, gaining information, and enjoying stories.

When I was in school, I was very interested in reading. Those days, books had to be either bought or checked out from the library. Now there are facilities to download books when needed and read on cell phones. We had interest, but no facilities. Now there are facilities, but no interest.

Even where there is interest, parents do not encourage it. They even prevent. Another time, a boy asked me, "Without going there, how do they measure the distances to the sun and other celestial objects?" He was speaking in Tamil tainted with some English words.

What a profound question from a twelve-year-old! I said, "They measure it using a method called parallax" and explained what it is and how it is used in this context.

As the conversation continued, he said, "For the tower of the Tanjore Big Temple they have just arranged stones and capped at the top. The cap keeps the tower from collapsing."

Surprised I asked, "How do you learn all this?"

"By reading on the internet here and there."

"Do you have any book?"

"No. Dad would not buy me books. He says I should only study schoolbooks."

"Do you read these in English, or Tamil?"

"I read in English and understand in Tamil."

"George Gamow describes the method of measuring the distance to the sun step by step starting from simple examples in his book 'One, Two, Three, Infinity'. This book is available in Tamil, too."

"I cannot read Tamil."

How cruel! Parents do not buy books for a child so driven by interest. They have enrolled him in English medium school, but he understands in Tamil. The fact that he is a Tamil child could not be changed. Children cannot read in Tamil; cannot speak in English.

8.4 Unbound education

Students of the same age can have different aptitudes and skills. But since one teacher teaches a class, the curriculum and teaching approach are the same for the whole class. When we use computers and software, teaching can be adapted to the individual needs of students.

At present education herds children into a room and tries to stuff knowledge into them. For children to become knowledgeable, they do not need to be within a particular set of four walls from a starting time till an end time. Their minds need a chance to read and think without any restrictions. You may think that being bound by a structure is discipline. This is not discipline. Discipline is taking responsibility for one's actions and performing it in appropriate times by one's own desire. Haven't you still understood that blocking people into a structure is an act of domination? In the old days it may have been convenient to gather students at a place and time to educate them. But there is also a chance for the dominants to misuse that facility. Today technology gives us ways of removing such unnecessary bounds.

There is the custom of going to schools and offices and returning at certain times all over the world. In the year 2020, there was a disease called COVID (Corona Virus Disease) all over the world, and schools were closed to prevent its spread. Several corporations asked their employees to work from home over the internet. Companies where work could not be done remotely were closed. Only essential institutions like hospitals remained open.

After COVID was over, many organizations continued to allow employees to work from home. The managers at these organizations had found during the COVID period that working from home was convenient for employees and the efficiency of work did not diminish. That is why even after the need ceased to exist, they continued this method. Even before COVID some corporations had allowed considerable flexibility and liberalization in how employees worked. Google is a good example of such corporations being very successful.

Generally, when there are no restrictions, employees work by their own inspiration. We see a trend of employees putting in more time out of their own interest in such circumstances. The work is also performed well. This can be extended to education. If students do not feel that they are studying to satisfy parents or teachers, and feel that they are studying for themselves, then they study with great interest. When needed parents and teachers can guide. Such guidance should not be scolding or punishing. It is difficult to inspire those who are not inspired by themselves.

Children should have the facilities and software to study from home. They can go to school or to a public place when they want to interact with other students and teachers. Students without facilities at home should be given facilities at school to study when they want. All must go to school for laboratory, workshop, and physical education.

The restriction that a given amount of education must be completed within a year is also unnecessary. That can be left to students' ability and desire. Then, those who can advance rapidly can, and slower students can proceed at their pace without losing self-confidence and without feeling inferior.

8.5 Equality as social justice

Thiruvalluvar's "advancing as high as their mind allows" can happen only if everyone has equal access to education. Inequal education prevents people from advancing as the nature of their mind can allow. We saw earlier that nature of mind includes intelligence, orientation, and inspiration. If society's most skilled are in important positions, society will advance.

Under the current circumstances, those who studied in English in private schools are appointed for positions of responsibility. Upper class and rich people are the ones who study in these schools. Further, questions for tests such as NEET, JEE for entrance to higher education in medicine, engineering and other areas are taken from the curriculum for central schools where upper-class students are enrolled.

Then, the question arises why the government schools for the poor also follow the central curriculum. If that is done, it would mean that the objective of education is to succeed in these tests. Further, since the central curriculum emphasizes Indian nationalism, it is not acceptable to states. And yet, when the central government introduced NEET without warning, Tamilnadu government tried to change its curriculum in accordance with the central curriculum. Since this had to be done in a hurry, this attempt failed. As a result, now the Tamilnadu curriculum is worse than before.

If education were to be available to everyone equally, the practice of buying education with money should be completely removed from society. Private schools are antisocial. The government should provide quality education to all. Educators and other scholars should design curriculum and textbooks. The government's role should only be financial sponsorship.

In fact, people all over the world should receive free education. There are the World Trade Organization and World Health Organization. Where is the World Education Organization?

8.6 Global education

Of the subject matter for education, some are common for all people of the world. Some others are specific to societies. The theories, theorems, and calculations we study in mathematics are independent of the people studying them, whereas, people speaking different languages see their native language as the primary language and others as foreign languages. They can study the foreign languages they want.

A subject common to all people may be called a **global subject** and that specific to a region may be called a **local subject**. Mathematics, science, and medicine are examples of global subjects. Language, culture, and arts are local subjects. Some subjects contain global parts and local parts. Although the theories of economics are global, regional economy is local. Everyone in the world studies world history, and people in a country study the history of their country. A country's state or province has its own history. In culture, we see a detailed hierarchy of world culture, country culture, state culture, district culture, etc. Within a region speaking the same language, we find many regional dialects. Every region has its style in arts like music, and dance. In dance, there are Bharatanatyam, Kuchipudi, Mohiniyattam, Odissi, Kathak, Manipuri, Kathakali, Ballet, Flamenco, Kabuki, Tango, Bhangra, Rumba, Samba, Salsa, Chacha, etc.

Now we can understand why there cannot be a single education for all of India. The subjects common to all in India are a few. Global subjects are common for India. Indian history, and Indian geography are also common. In addition to Indian history, every student should study their state history and local history. With Indian geography, should read state geography and local geography. There is no such thing as Indian culture. There is no such thing as Indian language. Central governments create Indian culture and Indian language artificially. They take one language and call it the Indian language. They take one culture and call it the Indian culture. Central curriculum is based on these artificial concepts. It suppresses the diversity of India. Would any self-respecting state accept this? Would any self-respecting Indian accept this? Is it fair that tests like NEET and JEE be in this curriculum?

What is Indian unity? Unity is all Indians working together for the country's security, economic advance, and education. One language, one culture, one tax, or one education is not needed for this. Patriotism is good. Does it make one's love for language bad? Cultural pride bad?

Since there cannot be a single education for the whole of India, the constitution says that the central government and state governments should act jointly in education. The Central government can devise curricula and publish textbooks in global subjects. State governments can then translate them to their languages. State governments and local governments should be fully responsible for local subjects. If centralized tests are needed, they can only be in global subjects. Even then, centralized tests should be brought to practice only after all states have adapted to the central curriculum. Since it is not so at present, millions of Anitas without the courage to commit suicide are living like zombies in India.

8.7 Evaluation

If the aim of education is to get students acquire knowledge, what is the purpose of conducting examinations and evaluating each student? To find how much each student has acquired knowledge! Who is to find it? Whose benefit is evaluation for? Students, teachers, parents, or employers? Primarily it should be for the benefit of the students. It helps the student to find how much they have learned and plan the next step in their education. Teachers and parents need not know this. Their knowing this information cannot have any effect on student's learning. Such attempts are likely to make students discouraged. If a student voluntarily shows their scores, they can be complimented. That will encourage them. If students desire, they can compare scores among themselves.

After studying each lesson students can test their understanding by doing the exercises for that lesson. There can be comprehensive exercises for several lessons at the same level. Such exercises and evaluations should be helpful to students learning, not hindrances. Teachers should not make students suffer in monthly tests, quarterly tests, half-yearly tests, annual tests, etc. Those who score low on tests need not consider themselves inferior. Lily extends to water level. Long stemmed and short stemmed flowers are all beautiful. All are people.

It is natural for employees to measure the knowledge of potential employees. But we have seen that getting a job is not the only purpose of education. If a student wants to acquire knowledge to their satisfaction and then use that knowledge to engage in some profession, they need not demonstrate their ability to anyone else.

We saw that common evaluation can be conducted on global subjects. But it is not necessary to conduct them. If they are conducted, it should be ensured that all students undergoing such evaluation have had a chance to study the subjects. Only when all students in the country have access to the common resources, a single evaluation can be performed.

The mode of evaluation that encloses students in a room from the starting time till the finishing time of the test and makes them write answers under supervision is called the **written test**. This is the only evaluation method in practice in India. This is a good method for evaluating informative knowledge. Students memorize information and reproduce in the tests. It is easy for teachers to evaluate and assign scores to such answers.

Apart from memorizing ability, the extent to which students have understood theories, principles, and ideas should be evaluated. This includes interpretation, showing examples, summarizing, comparing, and explaining, etc. Analyzing what is understood after learning, utilizing it, and synthesizing from it should be exercised. Students should also evaluate themselves on how well they can describe and explain to others what they have understood. It will motivate them to extend their education to acquire these skills.

To broaden evaluation there are many other methods. Written tests can contain questions requiring small answers, essays, and multiple-choice questions. Multiple-choice questions test understanding and utilizing to some extent. To test understanding and utilizing without memorizing, **open book** tests can be used. For open book exams students can bring books, notes, and other resources to the exam hall.

To ask questions requiring deep thinking to prepare answers, the examiner administers a **take home** test. That is, students take the question paper home and prepare the answers. About a week can be allowed to complete it.

Another method is for every student to collect information on an assigned or chosen topic and present it as a **term paper** for easy understanding by others.

In an **oral test** teachers use oral questions and seek oral answers to develop students' speaking skills. Students should also train themselves to present **seminar**s at an early age.

Thus, there are many ways for students to evaluate themselves and for employers to select the most intelligent people. Do the people making educational policies not know this? If a rustic like me knows, they certainly know. Then, what is the reason they conduct tests requiring expensive training and involving memorization? You can think about this and come up with the answer.

9 Grade levels of education

People, especially children, are naturally curious. Education should fulfil this curiosity and encourage it. Education should not be imposed from outside; it should be absorption of knowledge by internal inspiration. Parents and teachers can help this absorption. Neither pushing nor pulling, they should walk along and guide.

As children grow, their intelligence and knowledge also grow, and they want to learn at higher levels. In traditional education it is customary to divide children into classes based on their ages to educate them. Accordingly, education is broadly divided into two parts. Starting from about age 5, twelve years of education is termed school education and beyond that is higher education. School education and preparation for school are further divided into preschool, elementary school, secondary school, and higher secondary school.

In an alternate education method, we saw that technology can be used to provide every student with the education they want at their own pace, students should be free to learn when they want, and evaluation methods should challenge each student to advance as much as they can. Classes determined by age are not needed for this type of education. When a student finishes a level, they can move on to the next by themselves. Nobody needs to stand guard and open the door.

Among children of same age, there are those who can absorb knowledge quickly and those who find learning hard. It depends on their mind. That is, it depends on intelligence, orientation, and inspiration. Current education has been designed for the needs of an average child of a certain age. When all children participate in such education, this education does not satisfy the more intelligent student; the less intelligent get frustrated. Hence, at every level there should be sufficient resources so that individuals can absorb as much knowledge as they can and sharpen their intelligence as much as they can.

Though students advance at different paces, education proceeds through grade levels. As children age, they proceed to consecutive levels of knowledge. But different students proceed at different paces. Parents and later teachers should guide in accordance with their natural interests.

Such guidance need not occur through students and teachers being in continuous direct contact. Different students need guidance to different extents. Some may need continuous contact. That too should be at the students' request. What I am saying here is that teachers and parents should create interest in students. They should not force them to study. We will see in this chapter how to create interest at various levels.

9.1 Beginning of learning

We saw in section **3.1** that language skills are the basis of learning. When do language skills start to develop in children? You may be surprised to find the answer. It begins in the uterus! Yes, a few weeks before the baby is born, the child in the womb listens to the mother talking and singing. How do I know this? Because researchers say so! How do the researchers know it? They (Satt 1984) by working with expectant mothers found that if the mother sings a lullaby often in the last six weeks before the baby is due, then after it is born it is comforted more by the same lullaby than a new lullaby the mother sings. Many findings like this together establish this fact. That is, the baby gets familiar with its mother's language.

You can verify this. An expectant mother can feel when a mature fetus sleeps and when it is active. Sitting in a quite environment, the mother can see if she notices any change in the behavior of the fetus whenever she sings a song. After the baby is born, try to notice a difference in the baby's reaction between singing the same song and a different song. This difference may be small. Researchers discovered it by working with many mothers under controlled conditions. It may be hard to see it in all babies by all mothers. Still, this is an interesting way to relate to your baby. There is no doubt that the baby in the womb is listening to talks by mother and others.

Next, let us ask when a child learns to talk. You may reply that they start talking sometime from one to one and half years of age. At this age children's talk manifests in a way you can comprehend. But children's learning starts before birth and continues after birth. Even before birth the baby listens to the sounds in its environment. They hear their mother's voice conducted through the inside of her body. After birth they hear the mother and others speak more clearly.

As the child grows, speech patterns start getting deposited in the child's brain. The child realizes that we refer to different objects with different sounds. If a child is shown the shapes of many animals and each animal name is said aloud over several days, then when asked 'where is tiger?' or 'where is monkey?', even the child that does not yet speak picks up the respective animal. From this we see that a child understands the meanings of words several months before it starts to speak.

Now, think about in which language the sounds heard by the child are. Naturally it is the local language where the child lives. For those who live in Tamilnadu they are Tamil sounds. Suppose someone wishes their child to know English and speaks only in English to the child. But how do they speak with others? The child is listening to that too! If you want your child to speak in English, then you should rear them in an English-speaking society. For all children growing up in Tamilnadu English is a foreign language.

If parents speak in one language to tomato vendors, laundry personnel, and milk vendors, and in another to the child, the thought that the child is different from those people gets deposited in the child's mind. This causes division among people. Without your knowledge you are seeding stratification and hatred in that tender mind. The flip side of this is that the children of tomato vendors, laundry personnel, milk vendors grow up with the idea that they are inferior. If one day after your child grows into an adult, they are in an accident and are lying on the road, the 'other' children will run away with jewelry. 'This person belongs to the other class. Let them go to …' will be the dominant thought.

Whether you like it or not, the native language settles in the child's mind. An attempt to change it only creates the feeling that they are different. Equal access to education upholds equality in society. Furthermore, we saw earlier that education being in a foreign language or foreign style stands separated from life.

9.2 Preschool education

Education starts several years before children start going to school. In fact, humans keep learning from birth to death. Parents are the first teachers. Other family members are associate teachers. You may notice that the baby looks at your face with curiosity when you say, "Ah, Ee, Oo, Ae, I, Oh, Ow…". It makes a mental note of the different configuration of our mouth and its movements when we utter these sounds. This knowledge helps later when the baby begins to talk.

Next, we should utter sounds like Ka, Tha, Pa, Ma and simple words like காக்கா, தாத்தா, பாப்பா, அம்மா, அப்பா. These sounds settle in the child's brain at a very young age and help in brain growth and intellectual development.

You should sing lullabies and other songs starting from the birth of the baby. For this, you don't need to be a great singer or music expert or possess a sweet voice. You just voice songs with a simple rhythm while tapping the child with the same rhythm. This helps the baby sleep as well as develop language skills. Alternatively, melodic lullabies can be sung while swinging the baby in a cradle. Remember these songs imbed deeply in the brain when they are in the native language. In Tamil there are many songs like 'நிலா நிலா ஓடிவா', 'காக்கா கண்ணுக்கு மகைகொண்டுவா' for this purpose.

You can read books with large pictures and simple words. When we read to them, babies want to hold the books and play with them. There are suitable board books in English which do not tear in baby's hands. Due to the negligence of Tamil people, there are no books in Tamil for this purpose. Tamil scholars should create such books in Tamil and Tamil people should welcome and use them. As babies grow, we can read stories for them. If you point the words with your fingers while reading, babies will realize that the letters in the book are related to the sounds and their meanings. Remember all these activities are started before the baby starts to talk.

At first babies make meaningless sounds. Watching adults talk they try to mimic the sounds. Then they start uttering sounds with meaning even if they do not coincide with words used by adults. Since the mouth moves as if saying 'Um' while drinking milk and eating, while hungry many babies make that sound. In many families, words like ummum, yum yum, mummum become baby words for food. Since mother feeds whenever babies are hungry, babies view mother as food in the beginning. In many languages, the words for mother arise from sounds like um and mum. Thus, அம்மா becomes baby's first meaningful word.

When children start to speak words and small sentences, they should have opportunities to play not only with parents, but also with other children and adults in the neighborhood. Such social interactions are an important part of education.

After children have started to talk to some extent, you can point to letters on printed books or on screen and utter their sounds. Since Tamil is a phonemic language, there is direct relation between letters and sounds. Meanwhile, reading stories should continue. In the future all books including children's books are going to be digital. Scholars should create the necessary software. There should be software to show letters one by one on computers and cell phones and play their sounds.

We see that children take interest in playing video games on computer and cell phones. This is a natural interest in them. We can use this interest for educational purposes. Saying "don't play, study" and trying to redirect them only makes them dislike studying. Instead, why don't we say, "Gain knowledge by playing"? Why not convert education into a play? For example, sounding a word like படம், we can ask them to find the letters in it. After the child selects the first letter out of many given choices, the subsequent letters can be presented.

In addition to playing with computer, we can create games to play with other students, parents, and teachers. Instead of asking children, "Finished your homework?" or commanding "Finish it", think about how happy children would be on hearing the invitation "Come, let us play". Even if they know that this play is related to education, they will be happy. In other words, education should be pleasurable to them.

9.3 Elementary education

We saw that education starts even before birth. Elementary education denotes children starting to read and then write after they have started talking well.

Children get interested in talking first. Then we should teach them reading skills. We can read stories in Tamil with simple words. Scholars should create such books in Tamil. Parents and teachers should create interest in children to read by themselves.

We saw in the previous section that finding the letters in a word can be a game. We can show videos too. We can animate letters and show how words arise when they combine. Remember that Tamil is a phonemic language. The sounds of words arise by the combination of letter sounds. We can attach humanlike personalities to letters and digits and make them say their sounds. For example, the letter ப (pa) can introduce itself as "Good day! My name is பகரம். I make the pa sound in words. See, in படம் I am the first letter. In பம்பரம் I come twice once in the beginning and again in the middle". As it is saying this, the two letters one after the other can be shown by movement, growing bigger, or brightening. Hey, I am an old man. This is how much I can think of. There are numerous young scholars in Tamilnadu who have grown up with these technologies. Using their imagination, they can create any number of stories to attract children.

One of the characters in these stories likes numbers. She has the habit of counting things. While in a room, she counts how many lamps there are, how many chairs, how many plates in the kitchen, etc. There can be another character who likes a kind of letters, say த, தா, தி, etc. Wherever these letters are seen he points them out. Another one likes the ஏ sound. He is seduced by the letters கே, சே, வே, etc. All this may sound silly to you, but not to children. Teachers of children should be as imaginative as children.

Letters need not be introduced to children in alphabetical order. In fact, it is better that they are not in order. The alphabetical order can be learned at a higher level of education. At this stage, there is no need for the classification as vowels, consonants, and combinations. No need to teach in that order either. Children can see by repeated exposure that the series ப, பா, பி, பெ, பீ, பூ, ... contains ப in common and that the series கா, சா, பா, வா, ... contains the notation for a vowel in common; they can associate the symbol to the sounds. This is called **pattern recognition** in computer science. This is natural in children.

Starting this way, they can be made to recognize all letters. Then we can show them that words are formed from letters and ask them to read. At the next step we can ask them to read stories.

When they can read, we can introduce them to writing. With a futuristic view we should teach them touch-typing. At what age can a child start to type? There is no single answer suitable for all children. Parents and teachers should be watchful when the child is ready.

Children should practice on the Tamil99 keyboard from the beginning. I have said at many places in this book that we should write textbooks and other books of knowledge in Tamil. Clearly good writers are needed to write them. How can we create such writers? They should be trained out of children. They should practice, not only in the form of text, but also in the technologies used to create them. For this purpose, the Tamilnadu government should make available computers with Tamil99 keyboards and simple machines for writing.

We need software to make the machine say words and check whether the students are typing them correctly. Gradually the computer should take the students to higher level words and small sentences. When needed parents and teachers should guide.

Computers should ask students to say words and check them. They should check whether students' pronunciations distinguish between ற and ர, between ந and ன, and between ல and ள. Then prompt them to read longer sentences or stories and correct their mistakes.

I would like to point out that everyone in Tamilnadu at present pronounce ற incorrectly and they do not distinguish between ந and ன. We know that every hard consonant is associated with a nasal consonant and vice versa. The companion for க is ங. They appear together in தங்கம். Other pairs appear together in பஞ்சம், வண்டி, பந்தம், கம்பம், மன்றம். Whatever configuration the mouth is while uttering ப, it is in the same configuration for ம. The difference is that for ப the air escapes through the mouth with a little explosion, but for ம air escapes through nose too. You can understand it very well when you try saying ம while plugging your nose. Same thing is true for other pairs too.

Now, since ற and ன are companions, whatever the location and angle of the tongue are while saying ன should be the location and angle for ற, but air should only escape through the mouth. Notice that the tongue should not be bent backward. I am not saying this as my opinion. This is said in Tholkappiam. When I was a boy, this is how we said it in the villages of Thirunelveli and Thoothukkudi districts. Now even those in these districts pronounce it incorrectly thinking that it is civilized to pronounce it like the city people.

This way, we can realize the correct sound of ந. Just like for த, the tip of the tongue should be at the bottom of the upper front teeth for ந but air should be allowed through nose. If some have difficulty distinguishing between வ and உ, they can use the same reasoning.

When children learn letters, they should also be introduced to digits, numbers, and simple additions. This includes saying the numbers in order and which of two numbers is smaller or larger. The concepts of more and less are introduced. In the number list what comes first is smaller or less and what comes later is larger or more. Piles of different numbers of objects can illustrate these concepts in pictures. After knowing the numbers, they can add small numbers and then step by step subtract, multiply, and divide without remainder. Introduction to fractional numbers and decimal numbers as well as calculating with them are towards the end of elementary education.

While ordering numbers, ordering letters can be introduced. Just like in numbers, there are letters that come before others. Vowels beginning in அ and consonants beginning in க, and finally the ordering the table of all combination letters should be shown.

Students should tell and write stories from their imaginations. They should draw their thoughts in writing. They should write essays on topics they desire. In the beginning these writings can be one or two sentences and can grow over time. Numbers and calculations can be included in these stories.

Meanwhile, they should watch music and dance events to induce interest in the arts. There is an art called Carnatic music. There is another called Bharatanatyam. The smarties excelling in these arts output their arts only within the walls of a building at Chennai called the Music Academy. Still, several second-rate artists and progressive minded artists make their singing and dancing available on the internet. If possible, children can be taken to events taking place in cities.

At the end of elementary education, students should know reading and writing in Tamil well and adding, subtracting, multiplying, and division. Notice that foreign languages such as English has not been introduced. We will start it in secondary education.

9.4 Secondary education

The aim of elementary education is to make students ready for reading, writing, and arithmetic. Using these language and numeric skills they start getting subject knowledge in secondary education.

Students are introduced to many fields of study in secondary education. They can study many subjects such as mathematics, science, technology, and medicine at introductory level. Instead of reading from a proscribed book to answer questions in that book, they should have opportunities to receive knowledge in areas of their likings. There should be plenty of resources available for this. Such resources are not available at present in quality Tamil. This method of education can be implemented only after scholars create these resources.

There should be breadth and depth in curricula. All should have access to all resources. Students should have a chance to go as deep as they want into subjects they want. Each level of a subject should be the foundation for the next level. For studying higher levels of subjects, higher levels of language skills are necessary. So, language skills should also improve in parallel.

Children should have the freedom to explore subjects on their own. The question may arise whether small children have the knowledge of what to study first and which are higher level topics. Let us not forget that parents and teachers are available to guide and monitor students' progress. What is important is that this guidance should not be result oriented but should be based on children's interests. In a society where all professions are respected, and base lifestyle is accessible to everyone, there won't be result oriented educations. Students should be familiarized with music, dance, sports, and games. Only those who have the skills and aptitude for a profession would enter that profession.

English can be taught through Tamil to those who desire it. Those taking interest in it will study it better than studying in the English medium schools of present day. Students should first understand the differences between Tamil and English. There is a regularity in Tamil that one letter corresponds to one sound (or a group of sounds called phoneme) and vice versa. This is not strict in English. In addition to learning the spelling of each English word, one should learn how to pronounce it. Although sentence structure in Tamil is generally in the order of subject, case phrases (வேற்றுமைத்தொடர்கள்) and verb, it can be changed. Note that object can be considered a case phrase of the second kind. In English it is subject, verb, and object and it cannot be changed. The role played by case marking suffixes are played by prepositions in English; although object has no preposition and is determined by position. This is why the order cannot be changed. At present even teachers and scholars don't seem to understand or appreciate these differences. That is why they tend to speak and write in Tamil and in English the same way and cause confusion. They tend to write nouns in Tamil as separate words as in English without the appropriate suffixes. But this causes great confusion in Tamil due to sentence structure.

Starting from simple sentences, the same idea should be shown in Tamil and in English. This will allow students to gain skills both in Tamil and in English and understand the differences well. They will translate from one to the other language in accordance with the sentence structure of that language. Such scholars should be crated between Tamil and may other languages. They should act as Tamils' bridges to societies that speak those languages. In time machines can take over this task.

The present education tires to teach English disconnected from Tamil. It portrays English higher and

Tamil lower in status. Because of this, those who study in English medium schools lose Tamil completely. English stands detached like water on a lily pad. Except for some top schools, most people who studied in English medium schools in Tamilnadu do not know English properly.

In higher secondary schools, students start to specialize in subjects they are interested in. Here too there should be freedom. The practice of dividing subjects into three groups and assigning the first group to engineering, second group to medicine, and third to law should cease to exist. Engineers and physicians can know law. Everyone interested can know mathematics, technology, and science.

We have artificially divided knowledge into several departments. Now, we struggle without being able to solve social problems whose solutions involve knowledge from various fields. Universities try to encourage so-called interdisciplinary research. When the scholars in a society know many fields, that society can solve various kinds of problems.

I take interest in many fields, read about them, and use that knowledge in my work. After I realized that writers in Tamil need uniformity, I am involved in collecting technical terms from many fields and presenting at one place. Once when I came to know about compiling and composing legal words in Tamil, I talked with the person leading the effort and expressed my desire to participate in it. He asked me only about my education and degrees. Having told him about them, I also mentioned my efforts in technical terms. But he responded, 'you are in science, we are in law'. There is no chance that I may know anything about law. There is no possibility for legal experts and scientists to work together. He also mentioned that he has a Ph. D in law and another Ph. D in Tamil literature. He does not realize that certificates do not make scholars. He has a narrow view that refuses to go beyond certificates. Most of what I know now was learned during my career after I received my Ph. D. I consider a Ph. D the beginning of education. He seems to consider a Ph. D the pinnacle of education.

9.5 Higher education

We saw that the constitution mandates the government to provide free elementary education to everyone. In practice, in most of India education is free up to higher secondary. Higher education should also be free, because selecting suitable people and educating them for society's needs of engineers, physicians, and professors is beneficial to society. In that case, those who have the intelligence, orientation, and inspiration for these professions will take them up.

As of now, whoever steps forward to pay the most price comes to these professions. Having purchased education their first objective becomes recovering their cost from their professions. Patients may not be the first concern of physicians. Engineers may not be interested in the durability of the bridges they build. In contrast, physicians are likely to serve patients with money. They may recommend expensive treatments. More than what can cure the disease, they may be interested in what will make them most money. Contracts involving construction engineers can be associated with corruption, bribery, and low quality. These are the consequences of making education a business product.

In summary, creating physicians and employing them to serve society is a social activity, just like digging a well for the town. Even if well digging is contracted to a private party, the government should control it. If the private party digs a well as they wish and sells every bucket of water for the price they wish, those who cannot purchase it do not get water. Similarly, quality medical facilities are not accessible to many poor people.

It is expensive to offer higher education such as medicine. So, it is good for society and its tax money to select people with suitable mind for it (intelligence, orientation, and inspiration) and train them to become physicians. It is for this purpose entrance examinations are necessary.

In the educational method I describe here, this is the first time we come across competitive examinations for students to expose their skills to others. Till now I have been saying that students should study without competition. Still, they have been training themselves in taking examinations by evaluating themselves. Special training for competitive examinations should be outlawed. Everyone should have equal education and training. Examinations should be based on such training. Where there are inequalities, there should be remedies.

Only when there is uniform education nationwide, there can be a single nationwide examination. We saw earlier that not all subjects can be uniform for the country. There can be uniform education and examinations in subjects like medicine and engineering. But even here, how is it fair to conduct uniform examinations without providing uniform education? Examinations such as NEET and JEE at present are unjust.

Similarly, special institutes that train for examinations such as IAS (Indian Administrative Services), IPS (Indian Police Service), UPSC (Union Public Service Commission), and TNPSC (Tamilnadu Public Service Commission) should be outlawed and closed.

9.6 Liberal thinking

The youth of a society should have the maturity and attitude to realize, understand, and think about the issues arising from that and other societies. To think freely, their minds should be unrestrained. They should be released from social tethers.

The upper class has an interest in denying this freedom. They would not like the lower class to think freely. It is advantageous to the oppressor that the oppressed do not think for themselves and follow blindly what the oppressor says. It is natural that those in power provide an education suitable for this purpose.

History shows that such an education took place in India based on religion. People were divided into four kinds represented by colors. They had brainwashed people not to question it. They had people under fear in the name of gods and the concepts of sin and *punniyam* (redemption). They had immersed society in a belief system. Most of Indian society is still immersed in it.

Because of this, society cannot create knowledge by research and propagate it through education. This has prevented India from manifesting and subjected it to traditional obedience. This is oppressive education. Thus, all Indian students are oppressed. This education system prevents them from creating knowledge by research arising from their ideas according to their needs and interests. Their intelligence does not manifest.

An education that considers the good of all in the country should provide an ability to think freely for everyone. They should have the right to question the holy concepts that were not questioned till now. If they find truth in it, they may accept it; else reject it and break away from the social tethers it created. An education system of this kind is called **liberal education**. That is, it gives the freedom to think without restrictions. It gives the courage to think differently from conventional. We call this kind of thinking **critical thinking**.

With fearless thinking and new concepts people can undertake discoveries and inventions in science and technology and improve economic conditions. When not just the upper class, but everyone is involved in critical thinking, all of the human resources in the country is utilized. Society will prosper. True democracy will arise where all ideas are respected rather than most following the ideas of a few.

10 Equalization

We saw that if there is equal education in an equal society, scholars from all parts of society will serve society and advance it. But how to establish an equal education in an unequal society?

10.1 Stratification and diversity

Indian society is stratified in many ways. The stratification due to caste and religion is deeply rooted. Uurbanites consider rural dwellers uncivilized. The rich consider themselves smart and the poor dumb. The educated think low of the less educated. Office workers think low of laborers and farmers. Men belittle women. Thus, there are social strata in many ways in Indian society. A society which does not respect people as people is immature, unrefined, uncultured, and uncivilized. Quoting its antiquity and pride and patting themselves on their back is laughable.

In India there are people varying by language and arts. We call such difference diversity. This does not form a basis for social stratification. Since this shows richness in culture, it is something to be proud of. Governments today are smearing this cultural diversity and try to impose a single culture as the Indian culture. At the same time, they do not attempt in any way to remove the differences causing social stratification. In fact, political parties encourage such differences and try to utilize the situation for their political advantages.

Caste and religion too can be causes for cultural richness without causing stratification. That is, every caste can have their caste pride. In principle one can expect equal rights and responsibilities in society without giving up their caste pride. But in practice the upper caste does not give up their caste pride and lower caste are ashamed to mention their caste names. Hence, it is better we give up the dream that someday India will celebrate diversity based on caste.

Education should remove stratification and make diversity something to be proud of. It should educate that different castes have different cultures and there is no superiority or inferiority about it. Those who were oppressed because of caste should be lifted by education. This does not mean that the lower caste should be educated. It means that the upper caste should be educated that there is no inferiority or superiority due to caste. As of now the upper caste are uneducated in this respect. By the same argument, the educated, officials in high positions, urbanites, and the rich are in fact uneducated.

Once my fellow passenger on a train was a man holding a high position at a company called SPIC (Southern Petrochemical Industries Corporation). During the conversation he said, "Our people have no dignity of labor". When asked why, he said that the laborers working under him do not perform their jobs with interest.

Dignity of Labor is the title of a lesson I studies at seventh or eighth grade in my English textbook. This man who was of my age must have studied it too. In that lesson, laborers are trying to load a large log onto a wagon. Their supervisor keeps yelling at them saying things like "Come on, lift men! Is that all you've got?". At that time the manager of the supervisor happens to come there. Seeing that the laborers have difficulty, he lends a hand, and the task is done. The supervisor feels embarrassed for not having helped the workers.

This is the story. What do we learn from it? People in high positions should respect laborers' work. This is what is called Dignity of Labor. But what had my fellow traveler learned from it? He expects laborers who work hard for small wages to do their work enthusiastically and with interest. To him that is Dignity of Labor. The present-day practice elevates people like him to high positions. Am I not justified in calling him uneducated?

The upper class are proud that they are upper class. They expect others to obey them. A society with such polarization will fall. Because the lower class are also people. The self-esteem that everybody has is in them too. No one likes being suppressed by other people. This breeds only hatred. If someone from the oppressor class is lying on the road injured, someone from the oppressed class will run with jewelry. That is, the oppressed will be looking for opportunities to revenge.

The thought that 'This is us, that is them' can only create in society divisions and disaster. The feeling should prevail that though we are different by caste, religion, domicile, education level, profession, and economic status, not only we are Indians, but we are also humans. Education should create this feeling.

I said at the end of section 4.6 that if the situation of the world being polarized economically into upper and lower classes continues, the lower class will perish completely and the upper class will live happily ever after. But this is a dream of the upper class. This situation will not continue. Every society can tolerate inequality to some extent. But at some point, when the oppressed awaken there will be social revolution. In the upper class there are some with ethical principles. In the lower class there are some with courage. These two categories of people will lead the revolution. This may not be an overt violent revolution. Even now this revolution is happening and is having small effects widely. The sooner these changes take place, the sooner society will recover from the consequences of social stratification and start advancing.

The upper class may think that they are at unreachable height. Natural social forces will turn these differences upside down. The current upper class will suffer then.

10.2 The science of mixed marriages

In India marriages take place within communities. Here a community refers to a caste and a religion. There is caste among Indian Christians and Muslims. Because they are relatively recent converts, and they retained their castes. Sometimes some of them marry into another religion within their castes. Therefore, caste trumps religion. Thus, Indian people are segregated into pools. These pools do not mix by marital relations. That means the genes of different kinds of people do not mix. Let us see this in more detail.

Science shows that in humans there are 23 pairs of chromosomes. Every pair of chromosomes consists of hundreds of thousands of gene pairs. In every pair one comes from father and the other from mother. Because of this, in general, we say that 50% of genes comes from mother and the other 50% from father. This is why the child's features are a mixture of mother and father. We also see grandparents' features. Because it is their genes that come to the child through parents. If there is no blood relation among the four grandparents, each contributes approximately 25% genes to the child. Each of eight great grandparents contributes 12.5%. And so on for each preceding generation.

By this account, siblings have 50% common genes, two cousins share 25% of genes, and second cousins 12.5%, and so on. The percentage of common genes between consecutive levels is reduced by half.

The above calculations assume no relation among ancestors at the same level. Now, suppose someone marries a cousin. For this calculation it does not matter whether it is a parallel cousin or cross cousin. The couple has 25% of their genes common. For their children the genes coming from the father and from the mother are not completely different. At about 12.5% of the locations both genes are identical.

Everyone has two versions of the same gene, one from the father and one from the mother. There are diseases arising from defective genes. If one of the genes is defective, there is a 50% chance for that disease to manifest. But if both come from the same source both can be defective, and the disease will certainly manifest. In other words, defective genes remain concentrated when we marry relatives, and they get diluted when we marry at a distance.

In a society with marriages within a family or community, the defective genes remain concentrated over generations. In contrast, in a society where all genes get mixed up, we say that there is genetic diversity. Such societies are more likely to resist diseases and adapt to environments to survive and evolve. This is why scientists recommend crossbreeding over inbreeding.

10.3 Mixing in education

Treating everyone equal at least in education can be the first step towards mixing of classes. Social mixing is easier than class mixing. Everyone can participate in festivals, art events, and public meetings. In nearly all cities and big towns in America there are Tamil associations. All Tamils become members of these associations regardless of caste, religion, and profession and participate together in events, parties, and dinners. Schools, colleges, universities, and internet classes create equal environments.

Students are asked to wear uniform to school so that differences in caste, religion, and economic status do not appear. If we understand this objective, students will not wear symbols like caste string around the wrist, veil over face, holy ash or *pottu* on forehead; broad minded parents will not ask children to wear them.

The present practice is that although all students at a school wear uniformly, different schools prescribe different uniforms. It is easy to differentiate public school children from private school children. Every private school prescribes a unique uniform. Some private school uniforms include neckties, socks, and shoes. Thus, uniforms act as advertising for the schools. This defeats the fundamental principle of uniforms.

I said that educational materials like curriculum and textbooks should be common to all students of a locality. Even when it is so, different students have different family backgrounds. In the present system, there is not much difference between the school environment and the upper-class family environment. The ideas discussed in schools are familiar to parents in these families. Children hear them at home as well. But for children in uneducated poor families, studies end in school. Their lifestyle at home is very different.

Consider a family where the mother or father is an engineer. In the daily life of that family, conversations are likely to involve mathematics, logic, engineering ideas, scientific discoveries, etc. When these children come across such concepts at school, these seem natural to them. In contrast, children from families with only basic education find school lessons foreign.

People like engineers, physicians, and professors read books of knowledge at home. Some of them even have a small library at home. To children of these families, books, computers, reading, writing, etc. are familiar, whereas children from poor families see books only when they go to school. To them books seem frightening foreign objects. This is one of the reasons why I said in section 9.2 that books should be shown to all babies and stories should be read to them.

People of a certain high caste are at the forefront of Carnatic music and Bharatanatyam. In a way, we can suspect that they want to keep these arts to themselves without allowing access to other people. But children from other families also go to these artists and learn from them. In families already familiar with these arts, this becomes a part of daily life. Just like some people mumble movie songs while working, these people mumble Carnatic songs. Children growing up here listen to Carnatic music at home and at concerts. The chances are high for their relatives and friends to be knowledgeable in Carnatic music. Others do not have this environment at home. In their environment this music is not present. Carnatic music seems completely foreign to children in families unfamiliar with it. Even when they learn it at school or from a musician, it stops there. It doesn't come home.

By the same reasoning, even if children from Tamil families study completely in English, they do not know English well, because English is not present in their daily life.

We call the differences in habits of different parts of a society cultural diversity. These differences can be appreciated and enjoyed. But it should not become a basis of social stratification. Those who know Carnatic music need not consider themselves superior to those who do not know it. Engineers should not consider themselves superior to laborers. Even if there are different castes in society, there should not be notions of higher caste and lower caste.

The idea that a profession familiar in a family is easier for children in that family to learn leads us to birth-oriented professions. A carpenter's child sees carpentry from childhood. They start practicing it by helping their parents. Saying that a carpenter's child must become a carpenter for this reason is called a birth-oriented profession. By this logic, a barber's child becomes a barber, a launderer's child becomes launderer. Indian tradition not only assigned a profession to a caste but also introduced social stratification in professions just like in castes.

But what if a carpenter's child is not interested in carpentry? What if he or she is interested in mathematics or Carnatic music? What if a Carnatic musician's child gets interested in carpentry? Is it fair to determine profession and a social hierarchy by birth? In that case, how can one advance as high as their mind? How can society advance? Where to find people for new professions and innovations? How can science and technology flourish in such a country? Hence, even if there is no family environment in the studies or profession one is interested in, it is fair to create such an environment. This should be the objective of education. In time this will remove the birth hierarchy.

In this context, two Tamil movies come to my mind. In a move released in 1980 titled 'the color of poverty is red' (வறுமையின் நிறம் சிவப்பு), the son of a high caste top musician, not interested in music, studies a nonlucrative subject that interests him, gets pummeled by unemployment, and finally settles as a hairstylist. This very popular movie was later remade in Hindi and Telugu. In another movie released in 2023 titled 'Chef' (அன்னபாஐரணி), the daughter of a high-caste cook serving in a famous temple, though excels in cooking, wants to become a chef in a top hotel restaurant, and prepares chicken and other nonvegetarian items. This movie was banned after high-caste people complained that it insults their values. How the country has advanced between 1980 and 2023!

When I was a boy, launderers used to launder cloths by placing them in what is called white vapor (வெள்ளாவி). White vapor is nothing but steam. In the context of laundering, they call it white vapor. The expensive washers we import from abroad now have a feature called steam cleaning. The units with this feature are even more expensive.

Figure 1 "Automatic washing machines with steam cleaning technology are ideal for handling tough stains and deep cleaning" – The Hindustan Times, February 10, 2023.

Without respecting native professions of India, they have neglected to develop such professions. Now they buy the same technology from abroad at a high price. If all education was available to all, launderers could have learned technology and technologists could have learned laundering. Combining both, they could have designed washers and exported them to other countries.

Many companies arrange internships to provide industrial experience to students even while studying. This arrangement gives them the experience of working in areas such as medicine and engineering. Another arrangement giving real-world experience is the student exchange program. Here, students go to a different society to interact with students there, make new friends, and learn their culture and habits. In this program, students' parents in other countries host the visitors for food and stay. By this interchange students get a wide worldview. They gain an understanding and respect for other people and their lifestyles. This program immerses students of one society in another and brings them back.

Tamilnadu is a state with a diverse population. Every region, every economic level, and every caste has a culture. It will be greatly beneficial to immerse the children of one subsociety in another. They will gain friends different from themselves. They will develop an understanding and respect for different kinds of people. This will help students acquire knowledge, culture, and values they have not seen. It gives them a chance to understand and appreciate others' feelings and traditions as well as tolerance and sympathy where appropriate. A true democratic society will arise where people respect each other.

10.4 Assistance to the disadvantaged

Where there is no equality in society, even if education gives equal opportunities, we saw that equality exists. In such a society, equal education is not enough; An equalizing education is needed.

Even in families without high education, parents can devise many methods to create a suitable environment for education. I was born in a village to betel farmers. Both of my parents had completed the highest education available to them, namely fifth grade. When I was in elementary school, we did not have books at home. In those days, when you bought things from retail stores, they used to wrap them in pieces of old newspapers. After using the things and before throwing away the paper, my mother would ask me to read the words on it. My father would give me the receipts from the betel harvest and ask me to find the total harvest over several days. This way I was familiarized with letters, words, numbers, reading and interpreting outside school. For me, education became related to life.

The government allots reservation in education and employment to equalize inequality. Reservations are to be welcomed. But there is also a complaint that the unqualified also get opportunities due to reservation. To what extent reservation should be is a big question. It is difficult to measure the extent of inequality. In principle, reservation percentage should be in direct proportion to inequality. As inequality reduces reservation should also reduce until both disappear at the same time. People of all sections of society should move towards this goal. Upper caste, educated, officers, technologists, authorities, and scholars should sympathize with lower caste, uneducated, laborers, workers, and farmers, and take the initiative to provide them equal opportunities.

To handle social differences, we saw programs such as internship and student exchange in the previous section. To some extent, these programs can create educational environments for the lower class who do not have such environments.

We saw in section 9.2 that education starts in the womb and continues in babyhood. In section 10.3 we saw that some families do not have the environment for such baby education. Hence, teachers or other people with social wellness in mind should help children in these families. The government can establish nursery schools for this purpose.

At the same time, as we saw in section 6.3, a dominating government can use education to seed its principles in those tender minds at a young age. Since small children are curious about the world, they absorb information and opinions with open minds. The orientation they receive at this age designs their lives. It determines what kind of persons they will become. For this reason, parents should keep children under their wings as much as possible, and guide and orient them into becoming scholars. If they leave this responsibility to others, they should act after understanding the others' motives well.

The present central government in India is interested in inserting the Hindi, Hindu, India slogan into children at a very young age. They hide India's diversity and want to use education as a tool to make India a nation-state of single culture, single language, and single nation. For this purpose, they try to pull children to schools under their control at a very young age.

Traditionally children used to start school after completing five years of age. But the NEP (National Education Policy 2020) we saw in chapter 7 says children should go to school at age 3. In this context it is worth recalling the meaning of compulsory education we saw in section 4.1. It is not compulsory to send children to school. It is compulsory for the government to provide education to those who want it. Even that compulsion applies only for children between the ages of six and fourteen. Then, what is the meaning of the government coming forward to educate three-year-olds when it is not required to? Do they care so much about the poor and lowered castes? A caring government should attempt to remove the evils of poverty and casteism. Instead, it wants to release impressionable children from parents and take them into schools under its control.

Providing education to people is a social activity. Therefore, it is the duty of the government. But such education being useful to people is compulsory. Government should leave education in the hands of educators who care about society (not in the hands of businesspeople who run private schools) and accept only the expense for it. It should not interfere with designing curricula and administration. In such an educational system, scholars would offer needed help to children of lowered class when needed. In such a system, economically and socially backward babies will become familiar with the educational environment and adapt to it. Reservation will become unnecessary in education and employment.

But until that happens, there should be reservations.

11 What we do

Till now we saw how a society-based education utilizing modern technology should be. But education at present is far removed from that target. The remaining question is how to arrive at the target starting from the present state. This change can only occur gradually. Let us see how educational administrators, the upper class, teachers, parents, and the public can contribute to bringing this change.

11.1 Role of administration

At present, education is administered from top to bottom. Students obey teachers and study what teachers say. Teachers are controlled by authorities in the Department of School Education. Government organizations design curricula and write textbooks. Other government organizations conduct examinations. Thus, the ultimate authority for education is with the government. Because of this, whatever the government wants to feed the students is what the students get. Teaching mathematics, science, and technology is for the benefit of big corporations that support the government. Attracted by the desire to get jobs in such corporations, parents send children to schools. No one thinks about what is needed for society.

In a way, education need not be administered. Administration is needed only to control people and send them in a direction desired by the administrator. Such an administration is not needed in a situation where everyone can learn what they want as they want. Scholars should create educational resources and make them available to everyone freely and free of charge. Administration should only help with this. Granting and budgeting are the responsibility of administration. Educators skilled in educational methods should handle employing teachers and other such tasks. Even here, a deep administrative hierarchy is not necessary. Administration is something that helps, not controls.

Now, you may ask how to prevent and remove improprieties if there is no authoritative administration. But, in the authoritative method, what if the authority is improper? There is a democratic method for preventing and removing improprieties. For educators to check on themselves and on each other, **student feedback** and **peer review** are useful. Annually or with some other periodicity every student should give feedback on the helpfulness and other attributes of each teacher. The concept of students grading teachers seems an unimaginable act in India. But there is student feedback in all universities I have seen in America. The feedback on a teacher from other teachers is called peer review.

Democratic methods like peer review assume that most educators (or most people in society) care about society. In any society most are socially responsible and understanding. A few are antisocial. In such a society the majority identifies the antisocial minority and prevents them. If most are antisocial in a society, nothing external is needed to destroy that society. It will destroy itself.

Those who author educational policies should do it for the benefit of society. Here too, policies authored in a democratic way are beneficial to society. Those authored by authorities can be beneficial to the authorities themselves. Educational policies should not be static. They should represent a roadmap to gradually change education from the present state to the one described above.

As the first step of this roadmap, a few suitable students can be selected from each school and given the option of studying by themselves. A few teachers can be assigned to help such students from all over the state through the internet.

English should be an optional subject. Even if everyone opts for learning English, the option should remain. The situation can change over time as people realize the importance of knowledge. Those who are not interested in English can also gain knowledge by this option.

11.2 The role of upper class

Educators in a society should be representatives from all parts of that society. Sometimes, if historical events cause people from a section of society to be uneducated, then all educators may be from another section of society. In that situation, educators should not load their own values on all students; they should teach ethical principles applicable to the whole society.

Most members of faculty in the famous IITs (Indian Institutes of Technologies) are high caste people who grew up in cities. When India was under British rule, education was not available to people in rural areas and people of lowered castes. People of intermediate caste in rural areas learned to read, write, and numerical calculations in small schools. Hence, we can understand that when these IITs were started soon after independence its faculty consisted of urban high caste. But wouldn't we expect this situation to have changed after 75 years?

According to data MHRD (Ministry of Human Resource and Development) submitted to the parliament, scheduled caste (SC), Scheduled Tribes (ST), Other Backward Class (OBC) together constituted 9 percent in IITs and 6 percent at IIMs (Indian Institutes of Management) (The Print 2019). In some of these institutions there are no SC/ST teachers. The Print further quotes authorities saying that there are no qualified candidates from these castes and tribes. This is a lame excuse. The positions are a few, and 70% of the population belong to these classes. If they had equal access, it is likely to find enough qualified people.

If this type of situation should change, it is possible only if the influential high caste and economic upper class are willing to change it. Among them there are some true scholars who realize social wellness and the value of equality. They should work to change the educational system and social structure.

11.3 Role of teachers

In the alternate system of education that I described above, teachers participate only as guides. There is no place for authorities who force students to study. Starting from babies, students should be oriented to take responsibility for their own education. Without the need to satisfy parents or teachers, they should get interested in education by their curiosity.

This education system can be implemented only if there is a paradigm shift in teachers. Corresponding to the revolutionary change in education, there should be another in teachers training.

We should abolish the notion that teachers know everything, and that students receive knowledge from teachers on a one-way path. The teacher, instead of presenting knowledge to them, should induce students to think; should encourage to read books of knowledge on their own. There should be opportunities to converse with other students and teachers.

Students should not be afraid to ask questions. When doubts or questions arise in their minds, they should have the courage to clarify them with teachers or others. It is true that teachers should be knowledgeable enough to answer students' questions. At the same time, when they do not know the answers, they should admit it. Nobody in the world knows everything. Teacher posing questions to students as if the teacher does not know the answer is a technique to induce students to think.

The teachers at present have been educated in a system of memorizing, writing examinations, and scoring marks. Where to get the new kinds of teachers from? We can only get them out of the present teachers. Then who would train them? Well, they must train themselves! Otherwise, how can we create something that does not exist now? We can only create it from what exists. This change can only take place gradually. If government policies change, teachers will adapt quickly. But without trusting and waiting for the government, teachers can think about how to bring about these changes and can take small steps.

We saw that it is best to educate children in their native language. As a prerequisite to teaching in Tamil, teachers should know Tamil well. At present teachers for subjects like mathematics and science do not know Tamil well. They think it is not necessary for them and their students. This should change. They should realize that language skills are fundamental to education. So, all teachers should develop language skills in Tamil.

All teachers should learn Tamil grammar and good writing style and train themselves in writing clearly in Tamil. On that basis they can teach subjects of knowledge; they can encourage students to write and speak clearly. To write in Tamil, they should practice typing using Tamil99 keyboard.

It is completely new to teachers at present to get training in writing and typing in Tamil. We can expect great opposition from them. How can we encourage them to undergo such training? If you answer that the government should enact the necessary orders and appoint appropriate authorities to provide this training to teachers, you did not understand any of what I have been saying so far. An environment should be created where this interest will arise in teachers spontaneously. The first step is for teachers and people to get awareness. Scholars should exert efforts towards this end. Scholars together can bring about this change gradually. **Scholarly changes are stable; authoritative changes are unstable.**

11.4 Role of parents

Education today has boxed students within a structure of studying what the educators tell them to. It appears that the objective is to see that children's knowledge does not grow. Parents are the ones who truly care about their children. Children's intelligence should bloom under parents' embrace. Those parents without the resources, time, or skills can seek the assistance of teachers.

When there are resources such as textbooks on the internet, children can be left to explore the internet with parents' guidance. There are good and bad things about the internet. This is why parents' guidance is important. If children are taught ethics from the beginning, they keep away from the bad on their own.

But under present conditions, there are not enough resources in Tamil. Since children only have access to schoolbooks, they must study them. Still, parents should encourage them to acquire knowledge rather than scoring marks. Encourage them to develop at a young age the habit of reading good information and lessons available on the internet and in books. This will help them throughout their life.

It is important that parents give up the attitude that the aim of education is to get a job, and that they educate them with the aim of making them smart. They should have confidence in their children.

Please do not give excessive importance to English. English acts as a barrier that is difficult for poor children to surmount. This is convenient for the upper class. Let those who know English read in English. But those who are not interested in English should also get an education. You can find resources in Tamil as much as possible. Although this is hard in the beginning, as time goes on more and more books of knowledge will be available in Tamil.

11.5 Role of scholars

We cannot rely on the governments to bring about social changes and educational reforms. The scholars and other volunteers in society should undertake this. Guiding people in a society is the responsibility of the scholars in that society. If the 'educated' people with several English letters appended to their names are like 'ok, I studied, worked, ate, ...', what is the purpose of their life? What is the difference between them being born and not being born? This is the country where Bharathi lived, who challenged goddess Parasakthi by saying

தேடிச் சோறுநிதந் தின்று — பல

சின்னஞ் சிறுகதைகள் பேசி — மனம்

வாடித் துன்பமிக உழன்று — பிறர்

வாடப் பலசெயல்கள் செய்து — நரை

கூடிக் கிழப்பருவ மெய்தி — கொடுங்

கூற்றுக் கிரையெனப்பின் மாயும் — பல

வேடிக்கை மனிதரைப் போலே — நான்

வீழ்வே னென்றுநினைத் தாயோ?

It means roughly, "Do you think I have nothing more in life than forage for food, eat every day, chitchat, despair, suffer, cause others to suffer, gray, get old, and succumb to death?"

To the poor, who most of society are, it is hard to satisfy the fundamental needs of life. But there are many who have time for other activities after the fundamental needs are satisfied. Among them, there are many who sit in front of the television and watch serial dramas (soap operas). There are some who get involved in arts such as music, dance, and drawing. Some think about how the world started and how it functions. Some think about why society is the way it is and how to improve it.

It is the last kind of people who will bring the knowledge revolution that is needed for India. They will not receive any remuneration for this service. Nobody is going to thank them. Only volunteers who derive satisfaction by performing social services should be involved in this service. There are many such people who care about society. It is because of these people the society advances. Others benefit from it. Unavoidably, there are also cheats who derive the benefits without contributing.

நெல்லுக் கிறைத்தநீர் வாய்க்கால் வழியோடிப்

புல்லுக்கும் ஆங்கே பொசியுமாம் —
தொல்லுலகில்

நல்லார் ஒருவர் உளரேல் அவர்பொருட்டு

எல்லார்க்கும் பெய்யும் மழை (மூதுரை 10)

It means roughly "Water directed to rice plants while flowing through the canal seeps to grass too. If there is one good person in the world, on their account it rains for all".

Such scholars should create board books (section 9.2) for nursery education and textbooks for school children. They should write story books for children in Tamil. They should present higher level subjects such as mathematics, science, history, and geography in various formats, viewpoints, and cross-sections. They should present these subjects through many media including printed books, eBooks, audio for radio and internet, and audio-video for television and internet. This will prompt students to think for themselves. It will help them to analyze others' statements and understand various viewpoints. 'One subject one text' is a dominating authoritative approach. It prevents students from thinking in different angles; makes them listen to one authoritative source.

Scholars are few, and do not have the resources that the authoritarian government has. They do not have the authority or financial source for brainwashing people with propaganda on newspapers, television, and social media. But their statements have genuine values, and those values will be accepted over time. They should keep repeating the ideas in various forms. Constant dripping wears away the stone.

After scholars take the initiative and people accept, the government may realize this need and come forward to offer grants and salaries to scholars who create these resources. Then, other scholars who couldn't work without income may also join.

A prerequisite for all this is that scholars should give up working in the English language that they know and learn to write and speak well in people's language. Then they can write numerous books of knowledge and educate the public.

A time when machines automatically translate should arise in the future. But, before that time can arrive, the database (corpus) required for machine learning should be available. Machines cannot learn from nothing. For machine learning, there should already be many Tamil textbooks in every subject. Machines can only learn by reading these books. After that, machines can translate books, essays, and research reports that will be published in future. Hence, as a first step scholars should write many books in Tamil. Further, since what machines learn from these books will be permanent, these books should be of a high standard.

11.6 Role of students

In every section of society, some of the youngsters are very intelligent. Liberal education can make great thinkers out of them. They can carry positions of high responsibility that are highly meaningful to society. But at present when there is no liberal education, traditional education leads them on a single track and blunts their thinking. At the present state, this traditional education is a necessity to advance in life and to get to responsible positions in society. These intelligent youth should understand the situation and get traditional education. At the same time, they should see that this education does not blunt their intelligence. In addition to studying schoolbooks and scoring high on the examinations, they should read other books and develop various kinds of thoughts. They should not be afraid to raise questions and seek answers. They are the ones who will grow into scholars and lead the knowledge revolution mentioned in the previous section.

After learning in the present education system and becoming influential, they should take up removing the drawbacks in the system and instill a good educational system. After studying in English and acquiring knowledge, they should not forget that education in a foreign language is unfair to Tamils. They should not forget that corresponding to every educated person there are many who did not get educated because education is in English.

These intelligent youngsters, in addition to voting in elections, should take part in politics to seize government positions and bring a political revolution. For this, the public understanding the political system and voting for scholars is a first step. Sholars should devise methods for giving such education to the public.

When I said that intelligent youngsters are in every part of society, it applies to upper-class youngsters too. Those who respect social justice and who realize the evils of stratification based on caste, religion, language, and economics are there too. They should raise questions, at least in their own mind, such as why their parents enrolled them in English medium schools, why they made them not know Tamil, and why they were raised separated from society. They should take the initiative to remove inequality and other social injustices.

11.7 Role of the public

We saw that education is a social activity and providing it is a government responsibility. We also saw that governments use education as a tool to promote their principles. The government has authority and dominance. The government makes the law. Then, is there nothing people can do except obeying the government? People complain among themselves that the government and government offices are full of corruption and government departments such as police do not function properly. Do people just have to accept the *status quo* and tolerate it silently?

No! The root cause of all this is people!

In a democracy the final authority is in the hands of the people. The right to elect the government belongs to the people. This is what Bharati meant when he said 'எல்லாரும் இந்நாட்டு மன்னர்' ('All are kings of this country'). This is why the top officials in the government are called ministers. The people who are kings and queens elect ministers, members of parliament (MPs), and members of legislative assembly (MLAs) to serve the people once in five years.

But in general, the Indian people do not realize that they are the kings and queens. They see politicians as powerful and leaders, instead of seeing them as servants. The reason is that politicians have a lot of money to show themselves as big. There are ways to earn money to that extent in today's politics. Because of this, politicians view politics not as a service but as a business. They spend a lot of money to win elections and then want to recover what they spent multifold.

Just like we need to reverse education being commercial, we need to reverse politics being commercial too. Now businesspeople take part in politics. It is not surprising that the businesspeople in politics collude with the businesspeople in education. Seeing all this, why do Tamil people, in general Indian people, keep quiet?

Here too, the inferiority complex created by caste, etc. is in action. Society has created the notion that the public is good for nothing based on caste, economics, domicile, etc. But people of lowered caste, uneducated, and the poor have the attitude that the political system and the resulting governance belong to the upper class and has nothing to do with themselves.

To change this attitude, all people of India should understand the political system, constitution, elections to elect members of parliament and assemblies, and its consequences. Not only that, but they should also feel that they are responsible for it all. Since people do not understand this and don't have any feeling of responsibility, politicians exploit people for their own advantage and benefits.

When people are foolish, politicians deceive people, rob votes, and then rule as they wish. For true democracy to flourish, people should have the education for it. This is why I say that a job-oriented education is inadequate. Everyone should have general knowledge in all subjects like politics, economics, mathematics, and science. The present governments have an interest in keeping such knowledge away from the people. It is these ignorant people who have elected this government and will elect it in the future.

To elect a good government, people need good education; to get good education, they should elect a good government. When two things are dependent on each other this way, we call it a **vicious cycle**. We need to break this vicious cycle somehow. We should try to attack this cycle little by little from both sides. Good people should enter politics. At the same time, scholars should educate people as much as possible without any help from the government.

12 Conclusion

We saw that the aim of education is to make people smart and knowledgeable, and education is most effective when it is in the native language. We also saw that all professions should be respected equally to establish social justice and equality, and every profession should provide the fundamental facilities of life to every professional.

There is an illusion among people that private education in English is superior. But in fact, education being in a foreign language is a barrier to children acquiring knowledge; true intelligence and skills do not manifest. Private schools are in the business of selling education and making money.

Since education is a social activity, it is a government responsibility to make it available to everyone at no cost. Scholars should provide education. The government should accept the expense for it. But the present governments in India keep education under their control and feed children with the ideas and values they want to feed. Dominating education, they inculcate people with ideas like one language, one religion, one culture of Hindi, Hindu, India at a young age.

An education beneficial to people should stimulate people's thinking. It should be something students (in general, people) can acquire with their own interest without imposition from anyone. Without confining it to four walls or a period, education can be presented through various media using modern technologies.

There should be methods of students evaluating themselves on what they have learned. In addition to written examinations, students should evaluate their learning with open book examinations, take home examinations, term papers, oral examinations, and seminars. Entrance examinations for higher education and evaluation for employment should be based on education accessible equally to everyone.

We saw that education starts in the womb and continues in babies. When babies take various objects in hand, put them in their mouths, drop them, and hit them, we say they are playing. This is really education for them. They are trying to understand the objects and world around them. Education should encourage the same curiosity and leverage that curiosity to give them knowledge. Education should be considered a higher level of play. In addition to gaining information, students should be allowed to discuss and argue.

In a stratified society, even equal education does not produce equal results. Books, learning materials, knowledge and related ideas are in practice in upper-class environment, and therefore these things seem natural to children there. Since there is no educational environment in the poor and lowered caste families, help is needed from teachers and other scholars.

Though education is best in native languages, since there are no resources in Tamil and since higher education is in English, under current conditions children need to know English. But neglecting Tamil and teaching English starting from elementary school is a barrier for acquiring knowledge. School education should be in Tamil. Those who desire English should learn it as a language in secondary school. Only then students should develop skills in both languages. They will develop the future resources in Tamil. This will make it easier to educate children after that time. Very soon machines will translate between Tamil and English (any other language). Then higher education will also be in native language. There will be no such thing as a language problem.

But as a prerequisite to machines learning, scholars should write many Tamil books in every subject from elementary to high level. Since machine learning is statistics based, numerous such books should be released.

Today's students are tomorrow's scholars. Only if they learn Tamil attentively, later they can write good books, and make education easier, high quality and equal to future generations.

Today's students will also be tomorrow's voters and politicians. So, they should learn India's political system and realize the importance of elections.

An awareness should be created among the public, particularly among scholars, that education is the basis of all of this. If it arises in scholars, it can be easily conducted to the public.

References

Kar 2021; Kar, S. K., Rai, S., Sharma, N. and Singh, A. "Student suicide linked to NEET examination in India: A media report analysis study", Indian J. Psychol. Med., vol 43, p. 43.

"National Education Policy (Draft) 2019". Ministry of Human Resource Development, Government of India, New Delhi.

Nesan, J. 2019 "In Search of Education, Nationalistic Education vs. Society Driven Education". Indian Universities Press, Chennai.

OECD. 2016. "PISA 2015 RESULTS (VOLUME II): Policies and practices for successful schools", OECD.

Pennycock A., 2017 "The cultural politics of English as an International Language", Routledge, Tailor, and Francis Group, London and New York.

Rajya Sabha. 2018. Session – 246, "Unstarred question No. 1852: Source, Unified District Information System for Education", Delhi.

Satt 1984; Satt, B. J., "An Investigation into the Acoustical Induction of Intrauterine Learning" (PhD Thesis, California School of Professional Psychology, Los Angeles, 1984).

Sidhu 2006; Sidhu, G. S. and Jindal, R. "GATS and higher education: India moving towards global markets", The Indian Journal of Political Science, vol 67, p. 381.

The Print. 2019. "Diversity deficit in IIMs, IITs — just 23 STs and 157 SCs in 9,640 faculty posts", 13 February, 2019. https://theprint.in/india/education/diversity-deficit-in-iims-iits-just-23-sts-and-157-scs-in-9640-faculty-posts/191246

J. Kottalam is retired after serving in the scientific and technological research and development fields. He was born in 1954 in Kotkai of southern Tamilnadu in India. Having received MSc from Indian Institute of Technology at Madras and PhD from Michigan State University in USA, he worked at institutions such as University of California at San Diego, Scripps Research Institute, Harvard University and Cray Research with scholars including Nobel laureate Martin Karplus. He contributed to developing numerical algorithms for simulating the structures and dynamics of macromolecules such as proteins and nucleic acids in supercomputers. His further contributions are in the fields of Computational Fluid Dynamics and Statistical Physics. Now he is engaged bringing the scientific wealth available in English to Tamil in a planned systematic manner.

jkottalam@gmail.com
https://www.facebook.com/kottalam